First published 1992 by
Veritas Publications
7-8 Lower Abbey Street
Dublin 1

ISBN 1 85390 139 3

**British Library Cataloguing
in Publication Data.
A catalogue record for
this book is available
from the British Library.**

Cover design by Greg Millar
Printed in the Republic of Ireland
by the Leinster Leader

Contents

Declaration

The decree of the Congregation for the Propagation of the Faith (AAS 58, 1186 – approved by Pope Paul VI on 14 October 1966) rules that the *Nihil obstat* and *Imprimatur* are no longer required for publications that deal with private revelations, apparitions, prophecies, miracles, etc, provided that nothing is said in contravention of faith or morals.

The author hereby affirms his unconditional submission to whatever final judgment is delivered by the Church regarding the events currently under investigation in Medjugorje.

Interim Report by the Yugoslav Bishops' Commission (November 1990):

"In the light of evidence collected to date, it is not yet possible to affirm that events in Medjugorje can be said to be apparitions or supernatural revelations. However, the great numbers of faithful who visit Medjugorje require the pastoral care and attention of the diocesan bishops plus others, so that a healthy devotion to the Blessed Virgin Mary may be fostered in accordance with Church teaching. With this in view, the conference of bishops will, in due course, issue liturgical and pastoral norms. In the meantime, they will continue to keep the situation in Medjugorje under constant review."

Preface

Medjugorje found itself drawn into a further drama of an unexpected and tragic kind when, in mid-1991, the Yugoslav military forces, which were predominantly Serbo-Marxist, launched a full-scale offensive against their fellow-citizens in Croatia.

The toll in human lives and suffering has been horrendous. And refugees, including many children and elderly folk have fled in their hundreds of thousands before the advancing invaders; indeed, a good number found a ready and warm hospitality in Medjugorje and its environs.

The scale and savagery of the destruction wreaked by the Serbs simply surpasses belief. It was clearly their policy to inflict maximum damage on Croatia by wrecking hospitals, schools and public installations; furthermore, and even more ominously, they deliberately trained their artillery on churches and religious houses.

Satanic element

So inconceivably bitter and brutal, in fact, was the Serbo-Marxist onslaught on Croatia that it prompted several observers, including Archbishop Franic of Split, to conclude that much of its intensity and inhumanity could only stem from the powers of darkness.

In a word, there was a Satanic element in the attack and atrocities against a defenceless Catholic people. In saying which, we automatically find ourselves standing centre-stage in the Medjugorje drama. For its entire scenario is essentially, and from start to finish, built around the confrontation between two spiritual realities, two invisible totalities – the powers of darkness and of light; the kingdom of Christ and of Satan; those who fight under the banner of the Woman Clothed with the Sun or that of the Red Dragon (cf. Rv 12:1-18).

The flow of grace

It must be conceded, however, that, through the civil war, Satan has scored no mean victory on the Medjugorje sector of the battle-lines. For pilgrimages – those mammoth pilgrimages which so characterise Medjugorje – have shrunk to a mere nothing by reason of current hazards and restrictions. And this entails a severe blow to the normal operations of divine grace in that goldmine of grace which is Medjugorje.

Here we have but to think of the super-abundant graces on offer here to pilgrims from such a variety of sources: the non-stop flow of Masses and the emphasis placed on Eucharistic devotion; the central role of the confessional and the easy accessibility of spiritual directors; the spirit of prayer and devotion that greets you on all sides; the mystery of Mary, Gospa of Medjugorje, that is all-pervasive; the strong and vibrant faith shining from the faces of fellow-pilgrims; the austere appeal to Cross Mountain; the simple devotion and beauty of Apparition Hill; the peace of mind and heart – deep, divine peace – bestowed upon her pilgrim children by the Queen of Peace.

A second spring

We can confidently expect that, before too long, pilgrims from all over will come again in their millions to this sanctuary so favoured by the mother of God. But the indispensable prior condition is that the territory in which Medjugorje is situated – Bosnia Hercegovina – should be made secure against civil turmoil and strife of the kind that so wounded Croatia.

Meanwhile the spirit of prayer and sacrifice, which runs deep in Medjugorje, has taken on a renewed strength and vigour in the village and its surrounds. And the good local people are supplicating the Medjugorje Madonna to bring peace to their country and to bring back the pilgrims.

But the Medjugorje villagers are aware at the same time, taught as they are by the wisdom born of faith, that their patient suffering is a source of sanctification and purification. Thus they feel they are being prepared to play host again to the returning pilgrims more selflessly and graciously than ever, and to serve them with that love which is due to Gospa's pilgrim children.

Those happy days will come when the shadows of war lift from this land and Medjugorje resumes its role as a Marian shrine for all nations. Many a Medjugorje-inspired prayer-group scattered among those nations is beseeching the mother of God to turn this hope into a shining and lasting reality.

Richard Foley, SJ

Foreword

Medjugorje is a grace for the world. It has broken all records as a centre where confession flourishes, conversions abound, and the seeds of prayer are plentifully sown, later developing into thousands of prayer-groups across the world.

The grace of Medjugorje has been given for the benefit of those two decades immediately preceding the third millennium, preparing us for it in the spirit of Pope John Paul II's prophetic vision.

Mary, who brought forth the Son of God into this world, also plays a role in giving birth to him through the ages, culminating in his glorious birth at the end of time. Is the year 2000 close to that end? Or will it merely be a fresh stage, marking another millennium among many yet to come? The answer is beyond our ken. For, as Jesus has said, no one – neither the angels nor even the Son of Man – knows the day or the hour, except the Father (cf. Mk 13:32).

At the heart of a drama

The grace of Medjugorje lies at the heart of a drama. For the whole course of salvation, as the perspective of Cardinal Urs von Balthasar shows us, is dramatic. Yes, salvation history is a drama, not a cyclic and endless process of return and reincarnation.

Starting off with creative love, salvation history proceeds, after the drama of man's fall, towards love that is divine, saving and victorious. In the wake of that victory, the authentic drama of individual human freedoms created out of generosity by God, far from leading to nothingness, is crowned with the happiest of happy endings, namely, God himself, the fullness of love that is all in all.

The essential drama, whose dimensions are beyond our comprehension, takes the form of those multitudinous micro-dramas in which we ourselves perform in successive epochs. As for our own epoch, standing as it does on the brink of a new millennium, it is in a state of turmoil. It witnesses a proliferation of drugs, violence, and ideologies that are perverse and sinful. But where sin abounds,

9

there grace, conquering grace, is super-abundant. And it does so altogether amazingly in Medjugorje.

Multiple dramas

This explains the title of this book: *The Drama of Medjugorje.* For the place kindles drama of a multiple kind. To begin with, there was persecution by the atheist government, which later adopted a peaceful stance – and has since departed the scene.

But the Medjugorje dramas are principally focused on individual conversions and the collective tensions arising from the sheer richness of God's gift, the scale of which recalls the Acts of the Apostles.

Medjugorje drama springs, too, from the menace posed by Satan, who naturally projects a high profile in a place which so threatens his kingdom. Medjugorje may be likened to a microcosm in which we witness, in concentrated form, the drama being played out within the macrocosm of today's world, where good and evil are locked ever more intensely in a duel as formidable as it is mysterious. In other words, the spiritual combat being waged inside that circle of hills whence Medjugorje draws its name takes on, by an irresistible process, the dimensions of the world-wide struggle.

Fr Richard Foley, SJ

One of the outstanding players on the stage of the Medjugorje drama is Fr Richard Foley. This devoted Jesuit servant of Our Lady is well-known on both sides of the Atlantic as a lecturer, preacher and writer. He brings to his task a specialist training in theology and spirituality, plus a talent for journalism. Besides being founder and spiritual director of the London-based Medjugorje Centre, he is editor of the *Medjugorje Messenger,* which circulates all over the world.

In this inspired book, Fr Foley does not treat so much of Medjugorje's lesser aspects and diverse facts. Rather, he deals with its doctrinal and spiritual sources. Thus he singles out some of the forces underlying the Medjugorje drama, such as grace, the great sacramental boom (particularly the Eucharist, which is so central there), and those invisible, little-known, but ever-active performers: angels and demons.

In his final chapter, he writes in a prophetic perspective about the final outcome of the drama: eternal happiness in the City of God.

Modern man

Modern man is so conditioned that he lives from day to day like an ephemeral animal, oblivious of death and the life to come. More and more he resorts to tranquillisers in order to enjoy in peace the small comforts that fill his life.

But God, who created man in love and for love, has placed in his heart an infinite thirst – a thirst which God alone can fully satisfy beyond this time-world. Fr Foley's book sets our sights on that world beyond the present one.

Throughout the drama of our lives here on earth, Mary preserves us from hell, purifies us, fortifies us, and guides us, through her message of reconciliation, towards peace – and that happiness which is God himself.

René Laurentin

Introduction

In offering this series of reflections on Medjugorje events and messages, I realise that, for a number of readers, the world of private revelation, to which Medjugorje belongs, will be relatively unfamiliar territory.

I shall return to this presently. But let me first assure such readers that the Medjugorje world is most inviting and holy; to it we may with good reason apply what St Augustine said of the City of God: its very atmosphere is peace – divine, heavenly peace.

This lowly little village near the Dalmatian coast, which has become known the world over for its pilgrim multitudes, witnesses to the belief that Mary – mother of the Prince of Peace – is appearing here with a message of peace. Visitors will tell you of Medjugorje's messages, its prophecies, its signs; but, above all, they will testify to the place's evident sanctifying effects on those going there on pilgrimage.

Of all the many accolades presented to Medjugorje by devotees, none is more to be prized than the one coming from Cardinal Hans Urs von Balthasar. "Medjugorje's theology", he said, "rings true. I am convinced of its truth. And everything is authentic in a Catholic sense. What is happening there is so evident, so convincing."

Private revelation

Medjugorje is essentially the product of private revelation – of the prophetic kind. That is to say, it aims to benefit not only its recipients but others besides; indeed, Medjugorje's immense outreach embraces all contemporary humanity. True to its status and role as an instrument of private revelation, Medjugorje simply seeks variously to remind, prompt, counsel, guide, inspire, exhort and encourage the Church in her task of bringing to today's world the precious contents of public revelation – namely, the deposit of faith handed down to us from the apostles.

This same Church, let us remind ourselves, allows us to share with others the contents of any private revelation (apparitions, messages, prophecies, miracles, signs, etc.) without our having to seek her prior and express permission. The sole proviso laid down by the Church is that none of this material should offend against faith or morals (cf. Declaration, p.5).

In this connection it is pertinent to point out that, had there been grounds for the slightest suspicion of anything offensive to faith or morals about Medjugorje, the Church would scarcely have allowed it to continue on such a massive scale, and for over ten years, as a spiritual focus for faithful from far and wide.

Norms and guidelines
Medjugorje being essentially a matter of private revelation, a further – and all-important – consideration needs to be addressed. Because private revelation as such is a highly complex area even for professional theologians, certain norms and guidelines are called for in interpreting and evaluating the facts and communications it presents us with.

The apparitions
To begin with, the Medjugorje apparitions. In seeing the Mother of God as a three-dimensional presence, the visionaries are perceiving and experiencing something of that divine, eternal world which (for them) temporarily supersedes everyday terrestrial realities. So their apprehension of supernatural realities clearly has modalities different from those operative in ordinary knowledge. Even the likes of Teresa of Avila and John of the Cross had problems in communicating such experiences adequately and clearly. How much more, then, is this bound to apply to six young Croatians from a rural culture and with very modest intellectual attainments.

Their visions
The same factor bears on the visions of heaven, hell and purgatory reported by the young seers; they have also been shown something of the wounded Christ of Good Friday, while angels frequently

accompany the mother of God. René Laurentin, an outstanding authority in these matters, helps us to see them in clearer perspective. A certain degree of relativism, he points out, is bound to enter into all such reports, given "the role that interpretation and personal filtering can play". He stresses the need to make large allowance in each case for variables such as intellectual equipment, temperamental qualities, inherited traditions, cultural and educational background. Moreover, he adds, God adapts the object of the vision to the psychology and pictorial imagery of the seers in question. Laurentin sums things up as follows: "When invisible realities become visible, it is a limited communication in sign, made for teaching, and addressed to a particular time, place and audience. Those who receive this communication are not removed from their earthly situation nor their subjectivity."

Even St Augustine, himself the recipient of mystical experiences, was forced to admit: "Thy invisible things, understood by those that are made, I saw indeed, but was not able to fix my gaze thereon. My weakness was beaten back, and I was reduced to my ordinary experience."

The messages
Similar considerations apply to the communications received and transmitted by the visionaries. Fr Robert Faricy, SJ, who has written extensively about Medjugorje, observes: "Like all prophetic messages, those of Medjugorje are subject to discernment. As in any prophecy, unauthentic elements can creep into the messages. Those who receive them might unconsciously distort them, or give false emphases, or add to the messages, or subtract from them."

Another well-known authority on Medjugorje, Archbishop Franic of Split, in his 1985 report to the Yugoslav Episcopal Conference, said: "Our Lady's Medjugorje messages reach us through the children, and there can be misunderstandings, because, due to human imperfections, they are not clearly transmitted. Each message and each fact has its own degree of the supernatural or of what is not supernatural. In a word, we must sift the wheat from the chaff."

14

We should bear this in mind, therefore, with regard to the various messages issuing from Medjugorje. While we are perfectly free to believe that their source is Our Lady, we cannot attribute verbal inerrancy to them, as is the case with inspired Scripture. The Irish Mariologist, Fr Michael O'Carroll, CSSp, likewise warns us that the visionaries may lapse or err in the process of transmitting messages from on high. None the less, like all the aforementioned authorities, he accepts that the Medjugorje messages as received by us convey substantially the content of what the mother of God wished to say on each occasion. *In the ensuing chapters, these occasions are indicated for the most part by a date reference within parentheses.*

Not only Medjugorje

Nor is this "communications problem" limited to Medjugorje. Indeed, it is endemic to all private revelations as such, including Lourdes and Fatima. There is always the possibility, as Benedict XIV pointed out in his classic work on the subject, that "unrevealed or even untrue elements" may be inserted by a quite honest recipient of a wholly genuine revelation into his or her account of it.

Indeed, Fr Augustin Poulain, SJ, in his monumental work on mystical experience, lists no less than thirty-two cases of saints and mystics (all of whose revelations were quite authentic and approved by the Church) in which traces of human error were found mixed with the truth. For example, St Catherine of Siena claimed that Our Lady had told her that she had not been immaculately conceived. St Gertrude maintained that Our Lord had praised the virtue of patience because, as a word, it combines *pax* and *scientia*. As for St Vincent Ferrer, he invoked private revelation when he stated quite categorically that the end of the world was imminent and that Antichrist was nine years old at the time.

The secrets

Included among the Medjugorje messages are some that bear prophetically on the future; they are popularly referred to as "secrets". The same norms as outlined above apply equally here.

This is not the first time, of course, that visionaries have been entrusted with divine secrets. St Bernadette received three at Lourdes; they were intended only for herself, and she resolutely refused to divulge them to anyone. The two La Salette visionaries were each entrusted with one secret (1846), while at Fatima (1917) there were three.

There is a marked apocalyptic significance in the ten Medjugorje secrets, even stronger than was the case at Fatima. Nor is there any incompatibility between private revelation and prophecy, as the Queen of Prophets has so often demonstrated in the past. There are ample cases of future events being privately revealed. One thinks here of the Emperor Constantine being shown the cross with the legend: "In this sign you will conquer" – a prophecy of his future victory at Milvian Bridge. One also recalls that St Ignatius was told in a vision that the Lord would be propitious to him in Rome, and this despite the opposition that he would have to face there.

Locutions

Locutions also form an integral part of the Medjugorje package. These are mystical experiences whereby God communicates messages to the recipient through an interior voice, either auricular or intellectual. The two girls, Jelena and Marijana, play an important part in this respect on the Medjugorje stage, and their messages are frequently quoted in subsequent chapters. Regarding their interpretation and evaluation, the identical criteria need to be applied as with the messages in general. The same holds with respect to locutions received by people like Fr Stefano Gobbi, founder of the world-wide Marian Movement of Priests.

While the Church grants us a generous freedom to accept and also propagate messages coming through locutions and apparitions alike (assuming, of course, that their contents are consonant with official doctrinal and moral teaching), we must allow for the possibility of human error finding its way here and there into the transmitted text. For this is a regrettable weakness inherent in the very

16

concept of private revelation.

Readers should accordingly bear in mind that phrases like "Our Lady stated" occurring throughout this book serve as a convenient shorthand to obviate in each case a tiresome repetition of the foregoing observation: namely, that, in attributing these words and phrases to Our Lady as to their source, we receive them as refracted through the human psychology of the visionaries and locutionaries in question, and as duly reported by them.

The way forward

It is worth noting that, even when the Church confers her official approval upon a private revelation, this by no means guarantees the inerrancy of all its contents. Church approval simply endorses the fact that those contents in no wise contravene faith and morals.

Meanwhile, we have good reason to feel optimistic about the progress Medjugorje is making on its way to obtaining Church approval.

In November 1990 the Yugoslav Bishops' Commission issued an interim report about Medjugorje. It reads: "In the light of evidence collected to date, it is not yet possible to affirm that events in Medjugorje can be said to be apparitions or supernatural revelations. However, the great numbers of faithful who visit Medjugorje require the pastoral care and attention of the diocesan bishops plus others, so that a healthy devotion to the Blessed Virgin Mary may be fostered in accordance with Church teaching. With this in view, the conference of bishops will, in due course, issue liturgical and pastoral norms. In the meantime, they will continue to keep the situation in Medjugorje under constant review."

Two main points emerge from this statement. First, the conference cannot as yet affirm Medjugorje's supernatural character. Nor, in fact, would this be entirely feasible, given that much of Medjugorje's private revelation still remains undisclosed.

The second point is that the country's bishops have come close to recognising Medjugorje's public devotions as a cultus arising from the apparitions. According to the norms laid down by the

Congregation for the Doctrine of Faith, this is a necessary preliminary to acceptance of the apparitions themselves, though one does not inevitably lead to the other.

Worthy of note is the fact that some eight or nine of the country's bishops, including Bishop Franco Komarica, president of the commission, have themselves been to Medjugorje on pilgrimage.

1

The Drama of Medjugorje

For many millions of believers, Medjugorje represents one of the most exquisite and exciting gifts God has ever made to the world through the hands of the Virgin Mary. Besides being an altogether extraordinary episode in modern Church history, Medjugorje is spiritually one of the most enriching. Seldom before has anything been attested so massively in terms of that sole criterion Christ gave us in such matters: "By their fruits you shall know them" (Mt 7:16).

Indeed, Medjugorje is a prodigy for our times. The mother of God's apparitions and messages in this obscure Balkan locality have kindled a mighty beacon of faith and love for the whole world to behold and benefit by.

The Medjugorje Madonna significantly styles herself "the Queen of Peace". For, her prime purpose in coming, she says, is to bring her Son's peace to our unpeaceful, sinful generation. And the first and foremost expression of this divine gift, she insists, must be peace of conscience, that is, peace with the God of the commandments. Thence his peace will reach out, shine out, from ourselves as its carriers and reflectors, into the world around us, beginning with our homes and workplaces; then radiating its gentle influence into the regional and national societies of which we form part; and even shedding its blessings upon the war-threatened zones of our fragile international order.

Where it all happens
Medjugorje is a remote, rustic cluster of villages lying a short drive inland from where the beautiful Adriatic washes the country's south-westerly coastline. And, as its very name tells us in the Croatian language, Medjugorje "lies between hills" – gently-undulating hills set in a rugged, rocky terrain.

Despite the widespread building and modernisation to cater for

19

the pilgrim multitudes – new houses, hotels, shops, restaurants, etc. – the original Medjugorje remains a loose sprawl of cottages and farmhouses linked by rudimentary roads and occasionally wafting a whole variety of farmyard smells. Generally speaking, Medjugorje strikes the average western visitor as being extremely remote and rather short on sophistication and modern amenities. Indeed, Mary Kenny's witty observation on the place in its early days still holds as good as ever: "Medjugorje makes County Mayo look like the Riviera!"

The spiritual drama

Yet, incredibly, this sleepy little backwater has been transformed into a bustling Mariopolis, a City of Mary. For, ever since that historic June afternoon in 1981, Medjugorje has acted as a magnet for streams of pilgrims from near and far. Their total over the first ten years is reliably estimated at around twenty million, including some thirty thousand priests and hundreds of prelates.

These multinational pilgrim throngs form the constant crowd-scenes in the background of the sacred spiritual drama being staged in Medjugorje as in a theatre. It is a theatre of holiness, faith, prayer, penance and peace. And it is taking place in millions of minds and hearts touched by Medjugorje grace.

In order to see this in clearer perspective, we first need to see something of Medjugorje as an historical drama; that is, look at its main events and broad scenario. Readers wanting a more detailed picture will find this in those books that deal specifically with Medjugorje's background and history. Suffice it here to give a general outline of the Medjugorje story.

The opening scene

On the afternoon of 24 June 1981, two local girls in their mid-teens, Ivanka and Mirjana, were out for a walk on the lower slopes of what has since become known as Apparition Hill. Suddenly, Ivanka saw, higher up on the hillside, the luminous figure of a young woman. "Look", she said, "it's Gospa!" (the local word for Our Lady) Shaken and bewildered, the pair ran back to the village. But they felt drawn to return to the spot that same day. This time they were accompanied by a few others; all saw the apparition.

The following day, a total of six – four girls and two boys, their ages ranging from ten to sixteen – spied Our Lady higher up the hill, and many eye-witnesses saw them miraculously drawn up to her presence in record time. That sextet of young people was destined to constitute the definitive group since known as the Medjugorje visionaries.

Over the next few days, large crowds gathered around the visionaries at that same hillside location; what attracted them there were in large part the brilliant, unearthly lights that flooded the whole area shortly before the apparitions.

For and against

The Communist authorities, fearing a politico-religious plot to stir up Croatian anti-government feelings, moved in fast and brutally in an attempt to crush the whole thing. The visionaries were harassed and bullied, as were people who believed them. Apparition Hill was placed out of bounds and patrolled by militia. The authorities mounted a nation-wide media campaign ridiculing and vilifying the claimed apparitions.

Next, the parish priest, Fr Jozo Zovko, was imprisoned on a trumped-up charge of inciting an anti-State subversion. Meanwhile, the daily apparitions went on regardless – in private houses, in fields, in the presbytery, anywhere that seemed safe and secure.

Finally, the authorities, realising they were fighting a losing battle, settled for a compromise solution: the apparitions would in future take place within the church precincts, not publicly in the open air. This actually served to strengthen popular support for the apparitions, which now became integrated into the Eucharistic liturgy. Hereby, too, the people's faith and Marian devotion were channelled, as ideally they should be, in an ecclesial and sacramental direction.

Once the news of the apparitions leaked out to the outside world, the floodgates were opened. Films and documentaries were made. Theologians and journalists found a ready-made feast in the amazing events. Medical and scientific tests were carried out by top experts from abroad. And pilgrims poured into Medjugorje from every corner of the globe.

The apparition experience

Our Lady presents herself to the visionaries as a three-dimensional presence whom they can see, hear and touch. They report that her arrival is invariably signalled by a brilliant light out of which she, as it were, emerges. Standing on a small cloud as upon a pedestal, she positions herself just a few feet away from them and a little above floor-level.

The mother of Christ looks like a young girl of eighteen or nineteen. Nor should we be surprised at this. Mary, having already experienced, through her body-and-soul assumption into heaven, the resurrection of her humanity into a paradisal condition with and like her Son, is now endowed with perpetual youthfulness.

The visionaries describe her as being beautiful beyond words and radiant with holiness. She is dark-haired, blue-eyed, pink-cheeked; and she is usually clad in a translucent blue-grey robe with a white veil reaching down below her feet, and with a crown of stars upon her head. Suffusing her entire demeanour is maternal love of the most tender kind.

On occasion, Our Lady appears with the Infant Jesus in her arms or accompanied by the wounded Christ of Good Friday. And quite frequently she is escorted by a number of angels. Also, as we shall see in subsequent chapters, she has shown the visionaries something of heaven, hell and purgatory.

Unique and moving

To be present with visionaries during an apparition is a unique and moving experience, though anyone viewing this on video gets a good idea of what actually happens. The visionaries start by reciting the Our Father together; usually at some point in this they suddenly stop praying and drop to their knees – all in perfect unison. Gospa has arrived! Their uplifted gaze converges exactly on the same point, and they become totally absorbed in the (for us) unseen presence with whom they converse soundlessly, their faces registering the usual range of expressions common in a normal conversation.

At some stage during the apparition, Our Lady usually leads the visionaries in vocal prayer, normally the Our Father, of which she intones the first words. They then recite it with her aloud, again in perfect unison. Following that, they resume their silent colloquy.

Being in a state of ecstasy, the visionaries are immune to sensory stimuli. In the early days, their apparitions would last anything up to half-an-hour or longer; but latterly they seldom exceed two or three minutes.

Medical and scientific tests
Experts in psychology, psychotherapy and spiritual theology testify from their respective findings that the visionaries are perfectly normal and balanced young people. And a wide range of tests conducted by medical and scientific teams firmly rules out the alternative hypotheses that could possibly account for the phenomenon. These include make-believe, play-acting, auto-suggestion, dream, trance, hypnosis, hysteria, hallucination, drug-effects, epilepsy, catalepsy, manipulation by priests skilled in sensitivity-training and group-encounter techniques.

As for the hypothesis that evil spirits are responsible for the events, this has been blown sky-high by the "holiness explosion" that Medjugorje has triggered off in countless lives.

The basic message
Quite simply, what is happening through Medjugorje is that the Panhagia – the all-holy mother of God – is, through an outpouring of grace on an unprecedented scale, deeply imbuing multitudes of her children with something of her own holiness.

Now Mary's holiness, besides being a reflection of her Son's, is drawn directly from his gospel and exemplifies its commandments and counsels. From this same source Our Lady drew her programme of holiness, that is, her Medjugorje message, which is broadly similar to that summary of the gospel as preached by John the Baptist. Very appositely, then, her first apparition took place on his feast-day, 24 June 1981.

Five items comprise her message:

Conversion: This stands on the one hand for our total commitment to God and, on the other, for sin's repentance and renunciation.

Faith: It must be strong, active, childlike, unhesitating, informed, trustful.

Prayer: Besides being regular, frequent and devout, it must be "from the heart", that is, meaningful and sincere. The Rosary, the Creed and the Eucharist are emphasised by Our Lady.

Penance: Hereby is meant the spirit of self-denial and mortification in all things, with particular reference to fasting. Our Lady specifically recommends this on Fridays (also on Wednesdays); and the "best fast", she says, is on bread and water. This clearly implies that there are degrees of fasting suited to the health, capacities and circumstances of individual people.

Peace: This is the climax and crown of the message brought us by the Queen of Peace. To begin with, it means, as we have seen, conscience-peace; thence its gentle dynamic seeks to influence every level of human life, all the way from our homes to international relations.

The message is effective

So what Our Lady prescribes is no soft and tender marshmallow; rather, it is as tough and demanding as the gospel itself. Yet, mercifully and wonderfully, her Medjugorje grace acts as the spoonful of sugar that helps the medicine go down in the most delightful way! Thus, millions of ordinary people who set out to practise Our Lady's message find it much less difficult than it appears; they also tend to find it tonic and inspiring, a veritable sacrament of renewal.

How else explain that so many Medjugorje devotees now feel drawn, as never before, to prayer, with particular reference to the

Rosary and the Eucharist; that their faith seems to have taken on an added awareness and vibrancy; that they are being called to be more generous with God in terms of service, self-sacrifice and apostolate; that they now enjoy, as was seldom the case before, peace within their deepest selves and happiness of heart; and that the mother of God has given them virtually a new lease of life and a fresh sense of purpose and direction?

The message is universal

It is on people of every age and background that Our Lady's message produces such results. As for young people, they surely represent one of Medjugorje's most remarkable and attractive features. For it acts upon them like a magnet; and many of them go on to make its message into the music of their lives.

Another winning Medjugorje feature is that considerable numbers of drug-addicts and alcoholics, together with other outcasts from today's world, find in Mary's message a gospel of healing and rehabilitation no less than of Christian holiness.

Nor is it only towards Catholics that Our Lady's Medjugorje message is directed, though they form the bulk of the pilgrim throngs. People of all faiths, including non-Christian ones, seem instinctively to find there a spiritual home. This accords with the Medjugorje Madonna's affirmation that every single human being, nobody excepted, is her beloved child; accordingly, she encourages us to show the deepest respect for members of other religions, doing all we can to forge with them links of love and prayer. This likewise accords with Vatican II's vision of a spiritual unity embracing the entire human family in and under God, our common Father.

Additional messages

In addition to her basic message addressed to all humankind, the Queen of Heaven delivers in Medjugorje specific messages to selected individuals, such as the Holy Father, the local bishop, priests working in the parish, and, of course, the visionaries themselves.

An important development began on 1 March 1984: Our Lady initiated a weekly series of messages given every Thursday through the visionary Marija. Addressing herself to the Medjugorje parish in particular and to believers everywhere, the Virgin Mary supplies timely guidance, direction and encouragement in the matter of living her basic message.

In January 1987 she reduced the rate of her messages from weekly to monthly, delivering them (again through Marija) on the 25th of each month.

Further messages, many of which are of the same general kind, are given through the visionaries during the late-night hillside apparitions which usually take place on Mondays and Fridays.

Since December 1982 Our Lady has also been giving special communications through a young girl, Jelena, who was joined the following year by Marijana. They hear the mother of God's "locutions", as they are technically called, but see her only interiorly, "with the heart".

Mary uses these girls as instruments and channels for the deeper work of the Holy Spirit, imparting to them much profound and practical teaching about prayer and the spiritual life generally. And, under her instructions, Jelena and Marijana have set up a special prayer-group comprising young people like themselves. One of its most important functions is to act as a model and exemplar for similar prayer-groups the world over.

The ten secrets

To each of the six visionaries the Queen of Prophets has been progressively revealing ten secrets – that is, prophetic announcements – relating to the future of the Church and the world. Once they have received their full complement of secrets (this has happened to Mirjana and Ivanka), they no longer see the mother of God on the same daily basis as before.

On the termination of the apparitions, these tenfold prophecies will be fulfilled. All that the visionaries have been permitted to divulge is that the secrets relate mostly to coming events in Church and world history, and include divine warnings and chastisements;

also, that one of the secrets (evidently the third) bears on the so-called "miraculous sign" due to appear, as a striking and permanent authentication of the Medjugorje events, on Apparition Hill. Miraculous in origin, visible, indestructible, this sign, Our Lady has promised, will become a rich source of blessings, including the gift of faith for many unbelievers.

The visionary Mirjana has been expressly instructed by the Medjugorje Madonna to pass on to the priest of her choice (this fell on Fr Petar Ljubicic, OFM) the contents of each successive secret ten days in advance of its fulfilment. He is then to fast on bread and water and make a retreat until three days in advance; whereupon he is to communicate its contents to the world.

This arrangement has clearly been planned by Our Lady almost as a public relations exercise, dramatic and even sensational, in favour of Medjugorje, as well as a powerful vindication of its genuineness and urgent relevance to our world.

Signs and wonders
Right from the start, a range of remarkable phenomena has been witnessed in and around Medjugorje by many thousands of people belonging to every conceivable background and nationality. So the first-hand evidence ·is as cogent and convincing as could be desired.

For example, brilliant lights illumined the Medjugorje area immediately preceding the early hillside apparitions. The sun has frequently been observed to do such things as spin, pulsate, alter course, emit a rainbow of colours.

The big concrete cross on top of Cross Mountain has often been seen to "lose" its crossbeam, or spin rapidly, or change into a pillar of light, or even be replaced by the luminous figure of the Virgin Mary.

Mysterious flames once sprang up on Apparition Hill; yet no after-effects could be traced by the puzzled civil authorities. The Croation word for peace – "MIR" – has been seen blazoned like a brilliant night-sign across the Medjugorje sky; and any number of rosaries have been turned to a golden colour.

To repeat what was said earlier, there is super-abundant first-hand evidence for all these so-called "secondary signs". Their function, Our Lady tells us through the visionaries, is to validate the authenticity of her apparitions and highlight the urgency of her message.

Physical healings

Likewise in the category of "secondary signs" are the many remarkable cases of physical healing associated with Medjugorje: they go back to the earliest days of the apparitions. Over four hundred separate dossiers are on record in the parish archives. Thanks to the initiative of mostly Italian doctors, a medical bureau of investigation, on Lourdes lines, is now operative.

To give some examples: An Italian woman, Maria Brumec, had spent long years in hospital suffering from a compression fracture of the eleventh vertebra, and wore a back-brace. She was cured instantly in Medjugorje on 8 August 1983. Subsequent X-rays of her vertebral column reveal not a trace of lesion.

Even more celebrated was the cure of another Italian woman, Diane Basile, on 23 May 1984. Born in 1940, this mother of three contracted multiple sclerosis in 1972. It brought on, among other things, irreversible organic lesions, complete blindness in the right eye, and incontinence both urinary and faecal. She was instantly cured in the room of apparitions; this included 10/10 vision in her right eye. Moreover, the perineal dermatitis caused by her urinary incontinence had totally disappeared.

Well-known, too, is the cure in August 1986 of Agnes Heupel, a German nurse. Besides being paralyzed on her right side (this produced lesions in the nervous system), she had a tumour on the lung and suffered agonising facial pain.

The state's attitude

As we have seen, the Marxist authorities tried without success to crush the new-born Medjugorje out of existence. But, once they realised that it did not pose a political threat, they came to tolerate Medjugorje as an inexplicable phenomenon that was here to stay.

Furthermore, goose though it might be in terms of Marxist ideology, Medjugorje continued to lay the most golden of eggs in plentiful supply!

This is thanks to the ever-growing number of pilgrims who bring with them, for the benefit of the country's depleted exchequer, substantial amounts of western currency.

Amid the deep political unrest caused by the demise of Marxism and the breakup of the federal constitution, Medjugorje stands more than ever as a focus of peace, unity and harmony in a region so tragically divided by ethnic, religious and political differences.

The Church's attitude

Since early 1987, the formal investigation into Medjugorje has been entrusted by Rome to the joint national hierarchy, whose commission duly superseded the original diocesan one under the bishop of Mostar.

Ever since late 1990, the country's bishops have moved appreciably nearer to the first stage in the general process of approving Medjugorje. For they have virtually recognised the devotions associated with the shrine by presiding at the evening liturgy and praying in certain hallowed places such as the hillside site of the first apparitions. Indeed, even the Bishop of Mostar, who remains opposed to the apparitions, has likewise been chief celebrant at the evening liturgy.

But not until the Church pronounces her formal approval of Medjugorje will official pilgrimages be legitimate; those, that is, officially representative of some formal ecclesiastical unit such as a diocese or parish.

In the meantime, however, private pilgrimages are perfectly legitimate, provided that pilgrims are prepared to submit their judgement entirely to whatever decision is finally forthcoming from the Church. During Medjugorje's first ten years, hundreds of bishops and at least thirty thousand priests have been included among the twenty million pilgrims who, from near and far, have been to Medjugorje in this private capacity.

It is interesting to note that the Church's approval of apparitions (for example, Lourdes and Fatima) is, in fact, a relatively low-key exercise of her magisterium or teaching authority. Far from being a solemn statement at dogmatic level, the approval of apparitions simply amounts to the Church's declaration that nothing against faith or morals can be detected in the evidence as presented; hence people, motivated by human faith, are free to make official pilgrimages there.

Also of interest is the well-known fact that the Holy Father, while allowing the conventional canonical investigations to proceed in the matter, is personally most enthusiastic about Medjugorje. A good many bishops have reported that he has enthusiastically encouraged them to make a pilgrimage there, and so benefit from its copious blessings and graces.

Pilgrimage experience

Pilgrims warmly testify to Medjugorje's unique atmosphere of faith, prayer, peace and happiness. And its centre and symbol is the largeish twin-towered church of St James; staffed by Franciscans, it is now surely one of the most-photographed buildings in the world.

Another prominent feature on the Medjugorje stage is Apparition Hill, so-called because it is the site of the first apparitions. Then, too, there is Cross Mountain (Krizevac); it takes its name from the massive stone cross erected on the summit by locals in 1933 to mark the nineteenth centenary of the Saviour's death.

Literally all day and night, you see pilgrims making their way up and down those two hills. Climbing them is an exercise in penance as much as prayer, especially the steep, rocky path lined by the fourteen Stations of the Cross as it winds its way up to the cross-crowned summit of Krizevac some fifteen hundred feet above.

But Medjugorje's centre of gravity is very definitely the evening Mass. For this the church is jam-packed, the congregation spilling out far and wide outside. In warmer weather, a large bandstand-like pavilion behind the church acts as sanctuary; ranged around it in the form of an amphitheatre are seats to accommodate five thousand. At these evening Masses there can be anything up to a hundred or a hundred and fifty concelebrants.

Abiding impressions of Medjugorje include the long queues of penitents, with as many as fifty or more priests hearing confessions. You notice, too, and admire those devoted, hard-pressed Franciscan priests and nuns as they hurry about their seemingly endless duties in the service of the crowded and bustling pilgrim-scene.

Nor could you ever forget the faith and gracious hospitality of those wonderful local people who provide for the material needs of pilgrims from every country on earth.

The inward drama

So much for Medjugorje in itself – the theatre in which that tremendous spiritual drama is being enacted. Certainly many major scenes and acts are still to unfold, including the coming of the miraculous sign on Apparition Hill. But at a deeper level still – the level of mind and heart – the drama of Medjugorje is being played out a millionfold on the stage of conscience in the theatre of human selves.

Indeed, this is where Medjugorje finds its intended mark, its true home – our inward world of faith and prayer, repentance and holiness, grace and peace; our inward world where we meet the Lord of the tabernacle and the confessional; our inward world where we commune with God's faithful angels and do battle with his fallen ones; our inward world where we face up to such mysteries as death and damnation, purgatory and paradise.

Upon all these mysteries Our Lady of Medjugorje casts many an illuminating sidelight, thus enabling us to appreciate and treasure them as never before.

Here René Laurentin's observation on the mother of God's Medjugorje role comes to mind. "We had grown dead," he says, "and that is why a sign was necessary, to bring us back to long-forgotten truths."

Alas, some of these truths are not only long-forgotten but seriously neglected and in danger of being denied outright. This

31

explains, in fact, why the Queen of Prophets has kindled her Medjugorje beacon to illumine our faith, re-teaching us, in the process, several key, traditional truths that have become dangerously dimmed for considerable numbers of believers.

What the following chapters offer, in effect, are reflections upon a number of these central truths as seen in the radiant light shed by the Queen of Peace, Gospa of Medjugorje.

2

Fountain of Grace

Mary's underlying meaning is that she brings us both the God of grace and the grace of God. Besides being mother of the Word Incarnate, "she mothers each new grace that does now reach our race", as Hopkins expressed it. Thus Mary's motherhood embraces not only the physical Jesus but his world-wide mystical body as it winds its way down the ages.

What, then, is Medjugorje's underlying meaning? It is simply that the Mother of Divine Grace has dramatically transformed this lowly, back-of-beyond village into a spiritual power-house that generates streams of high-voltage energy and renewal for today's ailing Church and world. She equivalently says so in her messages. To designate a Medjugorje grace she often uses words like "great" and "special"; and she refers to the place as "a fountain of grace" (15 November 1984; 25 March 1987; 13 November 1986).

But even if Our Lady had not drawn our attention to Medjugorje's unique grace-producing role, this is evident in any case from its spiritual fruits. These are quite sensational. In fact, we look around for apt superlatives to describe the sheer scale and quality of Medjugorje's spiritual riches. It is nothing less than a goldmine of grace that the Queen of Peace has set up among these rolling Croatian hills.

Grace abounding
The workings of grace are omnipresent in Medjugorje. In a wide variety of forms you recognise its signs, its operations, its occasions, its victories.

To begin with, consider sacramental grace. Think of the enormous total of confessions that have been made there, each bringing into a contrite conscience healing streams of grace that pardon guilt and reinforce resolve.

Think, too, of the mighty volume of grace flowing from the

hundreds of thousands of Masses offered in Medjugorje by pilgrim priests. As for Holy Communions, they run into many millions. So Eucharistic grace is super-abundant and is much augmented by those large numbers who spend time adoring the Blessed Sacrament; this devotion is especially dear to the mother of the Eucharist, who has told us through the visionaries that she, too, is within that hallowed ambience and "special graces are received" (15 March 1984).

Special graces likewise attach, she has stated many times, to the Rosary. One thinks here of the myriad graces gained by pilgrims in this stronghold of the Rosary. One also thinks of those countless other prayers, all of them rich in grace, that have risen in response to Our Lady's oft-repeated plea that prayer – true prayer from the heart – should fill our waking moments.

In addition, she has issued a gentle but firm summons to fasting, penance and reparation for sin. How many brave and generous sacrifices this has inspired among her devoted children! Consider, too, the courageous, cheerful acceptance of God's holy will that grace has generated here in the hearts of so many sufferers and cross-bearers, leading them deeper and deeper into the precious secrets of union with Jesus Crucified.

More grace abounding

Think of the millionfold illuminations, inspirations, encouragements and good resolutions that Medjugorje grace has wrought in untold numbers of pilgrims. What is also very striking is the quite extraordinary effect worked by Gospa's spiritual goldmine on numerous young people. In a good many instances they receive the grace there to realise, as never before, just what a treasure is the gift of faith coming to us from its Author and Consummator, Jesus, Son of the Virgin Mary (cf. Heb 12:2).

Likewise meriting mention in this context are those thousands of pilgrim priests who have been bountifully graced by the mother of our Great High Priest. She stirs within them the sacred gifts they received at ordination, thus firing them anew, weak vessels of clay though they remain, to be holy and zealous servants of Jesus, Master of the Apostles and Lover of Souls.

One particular grace is extra-special in that it initially gave rise to the Medjugorje phenomenon and continues to sustain it over the years – Our Lady's daily apparitions; already their total exceeds anything comparable in Church history. And the same applies, Our Lady informed the visionaries, to the graces which they and others receive through Medjugorje (7 May 1985).

One very privileged grace received by the visionaries is, of course, the charism of being enabled to behold the Queen of Peace when she appears and to converse with her, besides acting as intermediaries of her messages.

Messages and signs
These messages, given at first on a weekly and then monthly basis by God's mother herself, represent a Medjugorje grace of the choicest quality; in fact, as she has expressly told us, there is no precedent for it in the annals of history (4 April 1985).

Nor would any catalogue of Medjugorje graces be complete without including the many wonderful and well-documented healings and cures that have taken place there. Furthermore, we are blessed in Medjugorje with a stupendous grace for which again history holds no precedent: the amazing proliferation of signs, mostly involving the sun, the moon, the stars, the cross on Krizevac, and numerous rosaries turning gold. This altogether extraordinary series of so-called "secondary signs" is intended, we have been informed by the Medjugorje Madonna, to authenticate her apparitions and drive home the urgency of her basic message.

This fountain of grace
In thus describing Medjugorje, our heavenly mother surely had in mind Jacob's well which features in St John's gospel. For it was there that Our Lord spoke about divine grace under the traditional biblical symbolism of water. "The water I give a man", he said, "will be a spring of water within him, that flows continually to bring him everlasting life" (Jn 4:11).

What we can equally apply to our context is the Saviour's remark to the Samaritan woman; she stood proxy there for our grace-needing, unappreciative selves: "If you but knew the gift of God!" (v. 10). Yes, indeed; if we but realised to the full what a golden gift Medjugorje amounts to – a fountain of divine grace! And if we but benefited from it as we could and should!

Amazingly enough, Medjugorje's future role as a flowing fountain of grace was, in a manner of speaking, "pre-viewed" by Sr Briege McKenna, the celebrated evangelist and faith-healer, several weeks before the apparitions began in June 1981. While praying over Fr Tomislav Vlasic, OFM, she received in symbolic form – as she is wont to do on such occasions – a mental picture embodying a message relevant to his spiritual life and work.

The picture in question was of Fr Vlasic seated in the sanctuary of a crowded, twin-towered church (the Medjugorje one down to its last detail, as she was later to verify). Fountaining forth from the sanctuary was a stream of water, which the people came up to drink in their cupped hands; thereupon, they hurried outside to fetch others, so that they, too, might come and partake of those refreshing waters.

This saintly priest was destined to play a leading role in the Medjugorje drama when he was unexpectedly transferred there a few months later to replace the imprisoned Fr Jozo.

God's life within us

"God is giving you great graces," Our Lady said in an early message, "but you do not comprehend them. So pray to the Holy Spirit for enlightenment" (8 November 1984).

The enlightenment we seek is not confined, though, to Medjugorje-related graces but should focus in the first place on grace as such – that is, on grace in itself, its nature, its purpose, its role. Only thus will we be in a position to comply with our heavenly mother's wish that "we appreciate the grandeur of the life God gives us" (25 May 1989).

The key to grace's mystery lies in that word "life". For this is literally what it is: God's life within us. Confirmation of this is found in that article of the Creed which declares: "I believe in the Holy Spirit, the Lord and Giver of life."

Through sanctifying grace, that good Lord elevates our human selves – everything we are, everything we do – to a level which is supernatural and directly oriented to its eventual fulfilment as the life of glory in paradise. And it is to the Holy Spirit that we appropriate the communication of this supernatural life, which comes to us as a sheer gift, unmerited and gratuitous. St Peter sums it all up in the text: "Through the gifts that make for life and holiness in us...we share the divine nature" (2 P 1:4).

No wonder, then, that this profound mystery of God's own life shared by us human beings is given so high a profile in Medjugorje by the full-of-grace Mother of Divine Grace – she who, in Vatican II's formula, "gave to the world him who is life itself". Indeed, the basic reason why she has come to us as Our Lady of Medjugorje is to ensure that we have her Son's life within us – and have it more abundantly (cf. Jn 10:10).

The supernatural endowment
In a general sense, grace is simply theological shorthand for the entire supernatural endowment God bestows on us at baptism. Besides being a sharing in the three Divine Persons' very own life, grace empowers us to relate supernaturally and intimately to them in three vital ways: knowing them through faith; trusting absolutely in their goodness through hope; and, though charity, loving them and, for their sake, our neighbours as ourselves.

This trio of powers accompanying sanctifying grace are technically known as the theological virtues. But over and above these we also receive a further set of virtues, each geared in a specific way to help us live up to our high moral calling as christened – that is, Christ-ened – brothers and sisters of the Word-made-Flesh.

Finally, and supplying as it were the finishing touches to this panoply of endowments, are the sevenfold gifts of the Holy Spirit. Their role is to render us receptive to the light and assistance of the Holy Spirit. Thus, as is glowingly exemplified in the lives of the saints, these special gifts make souls sensitively attuned and delicately responsive to the prompting and guidance of the Spirit of God.

Significantly enough, Our Lady has stressed how necessary are the Spirit's gifts for us to bear effective witness to her presence in Medjugorje and to the wonderful benefits she is conferring upon us there (17 April 1986).

Apparatus and actual grace

In the light of all this we can appreciate better what the mother of Christ means by the grandeur of grace. For it sanctifies and elevates us to the level of God's own life, the Christosphere; moreover, grace equips us with a remarkable range of vitalities and capabilities whereby we are enabled to live and move and have our being, already here on earth, in God's supernatural, eternal kingdom (cf. Ac 17:28)

All the foregoing elements comprise within us what can be described as an apparatus of supernatural life. But for it to be set in motion, this apparatus needs to be triggered off, activated, actuated.

This is the function of so-called actual grace. It refers to those myriad, transitory touches God applies to our understanding and our will, mobilising them to preform Christ-like thoughts, words and actions. "Without me", says Our Lord, "you can do nothing" (Jn 15:5).

This text confirms the absolute necessity of actual grace for each and every salutary act. The same point is made by St Paul: "For it is God who works in you both to will and to accomplish according to his good will" (Ph 2:13).

Temple of the Trinity

What we have so far been considering is so-called "created grace" – a divine masterpiece of immense grandeur. Yet it pales into insignificance when compared with that further gift God bestows along with sanctifying grace. It is called "uncreated grace" – precisely because it is the presence within the soul of the great Creator himself.

What this means in effect is that the three divine persons make their dwelling-place in our body-soul selves. Thus we become living temples of God, flesh-and-blood sanctuaries of the Trinity. This mystery of divine inhabitation was referred to by Our Lord when he said: "If anyone loves me, my Father and I will love him, and we will come to him and make our abode with him" (Jn 14:23). St Paul was fully aware of this sublime mystery. "Do you not understand", he writes, "that you are God's temple, and that God's Spirit has his dwelling in you?" (1 Co 3:16).

Grace's value

"The entire material universe and everything it contains", declares St Thomas, "is of less value in God's eyes than the grace present in any individual person."

Why this is so is plain to see. Uncreated grace consecrates the human personality to God, transforming it into a living shrine of the triune Lord. This stupendous grace clearly out-grandeurs by far even the splendours and marvels of created grace, since these are but the effects or reflections in the soul of the indwelling Godhead.

If we but knew the gift of God! "He who bears God in his heart", St Alphonsus used to say, "carries his paradise wherever he goes." Through grace we become princes and princesses of God's kingdom and possess its heavenly treasures. But let us heed St Paul's warning: we carry the treasures of heaven in that frail, brittle earthenware which is ourselves (2 Co 4:7).

This warning is echoed again and again by Our Lady of Medjugorje. She urges us to pray and maintain constant vigilance against the subtle snares of fallen angels. Also she tells us to go frequently to confession – a rich source of sacramental grace, purifying and fortifying in its effects. Above all, she directs us to the mysteries of the Eucharist, where, she says, graces of a special kind abound (15 March 1984).

In fact, everything in Medjugorje is geared to produce spiritual growth, which is identical with growth in grace. The Mother of Divine Grace earnestly wants us, in St Peter's words, "to grow up in grace, and in the knowledge of Our Lord and Saviour, Jesus Christ" (2 P 3:18). And, too, she ardently desires, with St Paul, that we be "filled with all the completion God has to give" (Ep 3:19).

The beauty of grace

Beauty is another of grace's qualities that features prominently in Our Lady's teaching. For example: "Pray in order to discover the grandeur and beauty of the life God gives you" (25 May 1989) ..."I wish to clothe you in holiness...so that from day to day you may become more beautiful" (24 October 1985) .... "When you pray, you become much more beautiful" (18 December 1986).

This chimes in with what traditional theology says on the subject. Thus St Thomas described grace as "a certain beauty of soul which wins the divine love". And grace does so for the good reason that it is the mirror image, the radiant reflection, in the human soul of him whom St Augustine extols as "the supreme Loveliness, the uncreated Beauty, the Beauty of ancient days". The man from whom St Augustine drew much of his early inspiration – St Ambrose of Milan – used to liken God to a supreme artist whose skilful workings with grace produces in our souls sheer masterpieces, lovely beyond words. It was suggested by St Thomas that grace acts on human spirits like a light suffusing diving radiance, transfiguring them with its heavenly beauty.

Beholding beauty

Of course, we cannot observe grace's supernatural beauty for ourselves any more than we can its array of vitalities and dynamic operations within us. All such realities remain concealed behind the veil of faith. Nevertheless, a number of mystics have been privileged with a glimpse beyond that veil into the sublime world of the supernatural. And their witness regarding grace fully corroborates the common teaching on the subject.

St Catherine of Siena, for example, relates that initially she had been totally unable to understand why God had done and suffered so much for wretched human sinners. Thereupon, she continues,

Our Lord appeared to her and let her see with her own eyes the beauty of a soul in a state of grace. "See," he said, "was it not worth my living, suffering and dying for something so surpassingly beautiful?"

Sr Mary Magdalen of Pazzi bears similar witness. If we were fully and clearly to behold, she declares, the entrancing beauty of a soul in a state of grace, we would surely die through an excess of joy.

The beauty of holiness, which is grace finding expression in the love of charity, was affirmed by our Lady when asked by young Jelena why she was so beautiful. She replied: "I am beautiful because I love. If you want to be beautiful, love" (25 January 1985).

As we have seen, the beauty in question is the reflection within their human temples of the indwelling Three-in-One who is the uncreated beauty, or in Hopkins' phrase, "beauty's self and beauty's giver". In a word, it is the beauty of Mary-likeness. It is the glow of immaculacy shed by her who mothers both the God of life and the grace-life of God.

Mother of Divine Grace

This title puts Mary's role in Medjugorje into very clear perspective. Having given to our world the author and source of all life, she now gives his divine life to the world. And she does so in her capacity as mother of universal humankind as well as of its creator and Lord. "I want to save you," she has made clear to us at Medjugorje, "and, through you, the whole world" (30 July 1987). Medjugorje grace, in other words, is meant to be as universal in outreach as Mary's motherhood itself.

In one of her messages, Our Lady is on record as declaring: "I am the Mediatrix between you and your God" (17 July 1986). Here she is affirming her spiritual motherhood in the order of grace and her corresponding role as go-between (this is what "Mediatrix" literally means) in its universal distribution. "Nothing is given to us from God's great treasury of grace," wrote Leo XIII, "except through Mary." Here he was simply echoing a whole galaxy of saints and theologians down the centuries. What they mean is that every grace is conferred by God thanks to Mary's motherly and intercessory cooperation.

So all grace as such is Marian. Starting with our baptism, every grace received by us over a lifetime has a Mary-touch to it and is fragrant with the perfume of her holiness. What likewise comes to us from God through his holy mother is every single droplet in that mighty fountain of grace flowing in Medjugorje for a world parched by spiritual drought.

To put all this another way: she who mothered Emmanuel is now spiritual mother of his mystical body as well. With regard to each of his members, she exercises her God-given maternal role. As Mother of Divine Grace, she accordingly presides over his birth in our souls through baptism, subsequently protecting and nourishing that precious divine life within us as we journey down the years. To quote another line from Hopkins, "Mary creates in us new Bethlehems and new Nazareths."

We might aptly add that new Calvaries, too, are created in us by the all-holy Virgin. For she presides as a prayerful and loving mother over the deathbeds of her faithful children, winning for them what the Council of Trent rightly calls "the great grace of final perseverance" – namely, the grace of dying in her son's friendship and peace.

Grace's wider horizons

Yet another aspect of grace emerges most strikingly and appealingly from Our Lady's messages. It focuses on grace's social and communitarian dimension. Hereby is understood that the self-same supernatural life makes us brothers and sisters in Christ, knitting us together into a vast solidarity that transcends space and time. This is commonly known as the mystical body – a spiritual immensity which extends across the world and spans the ages.

Also belonging to this mystical body are the souls in purgatory and the blessed in heaven (as well as the angels, since their supernatural life, like ours, is Christic). And the love of charity, by linking together all Christ's members into a vital network of inter-personal relations, brings about that wonderful reality known as the communion of saints.

All its members, be they on earth, in purgatory or in heaven, jointly possess and profit by the rich treasury of merits won for us by the Saviour, his mother, his martyrs, and his countless holy ones down the centuries. Through prayer and sacrifice, these and our own merits can be applied and distributed for the benefit of others.

Knowing this full well, Our Lady of Medjugorje pleads for our generous cooperation in her work for souls, time and again repeating the formula: "I need your prayers and sacrifices" (10 October 1990).

The response on the part of the visionaries has been magnificent. Mirjana, for example, feels it to be her special mission to pray for the conversion of unbelievers, and make sacrifices on their behalf (18 March 1991). And Vicka was expressly invited by the mother of God to offer the pain she suffered for the conversion of sinners, as is related in her famous interview with Fr Janko Bubalo.

Exciting vistas

Similarly, the Queen of Peace forges links between us and the worlds of purgatory and heaven. Indeed, on one occasion she skilfully brought in both, urging us to pray daily and offer sacrifices for the holy souls – and going on to point out that in so doing we would in due course win for ourselves fresh intercessors in heaven (6 November 1986).

So our Medjugorje mother is lifting our gaze beyond the narrow horizon of our personal lives to the exciting vistas of the communion of saints. We further learn from her that our own destinies are vitally interlinked with those of our multitudinous brothers and sisters on both sides of the grave; and, too, that we can become channels of grace for their helping and healing.

Our Lady has also indicated that it matters little how hidden or insignificant any individual may be, or how small and weak they may feel; each plays his part in God's plan by doing what they can according to their capacities (30 October 1985).

One thinks here of chosen souls like Georgette Faniel. Confined though she is to her sick-room, by offering her pain co-redemptively with that of Christ, she generates mighty amounts of grace-power to bring God's light and warmth into the world of souls, particularly her area of predilection – Medjugorje: its bishop, its priests, its visionaries, its pilgrims, its world-wide network of devotees and supporters.

Closing prayer to Gospa

O Gospa of Medjugorje, intercede constantly for us with your Son, of whose fullness we have all received, grace for grace. We thank you, Mother of Divine Grace, for the golden treasures you are giving us through Medjugorje. May we be faithful to them and generous in sharing them with others.

Win for us, dearest mother Mary, the grace of a close devotion to your Son in his Eucharistic mysteries and abiding presence in our tabernacles. Thou who art full of grace and beautiful beyond compare, fan the flames, the lovely flames, of consecration and ardour which were lit in the souls of your priests the day they were ordained. And inspire your priests, Queen of the Most Holy Rosary, to lead and encourage others in devotion to the Rosary, the daily Rosary – that rich source of divine grace.

Keep in your special and loving care, O holy mother of God, those pilgrim throngs from near and far who have been enriched by Medjugorje's golden graces. And bless all who believe in what you are saying and doing there in that fountain of grace, that shrine of your peace.

Pray for us sinners, Immaculate Mary, now – this present moment, this day as it passes – transmuting the dull lead of routine duties and trials into the gold of grace and merit. And pray for us, thou who art the Gate of Heaven, at the hour of our death, and conduct us safely to that City where grace is transfigured into glory.

44

3

School of Holiness

Right from the start of her Medjugorje apparitions, our heavenly mother has been addressing to the world at large, and to each individual one of us in particular, a call, a clarion call, to holiness. She does so as Queen of Prophets; that is, she speaks in God's name and on his behalf. Besides, she speaks not merely as mouthpiece of the infinite being whose commandments are to be honoured and obeyed but as his mother. Because he himself is holy, he has enjoined us to make holiness our aim (cf. Lv 11:22). Now his sinless mother is reminding us in Medjugorje of this imperative duty.

She is ever returning to the theme; in fact, "holiness" runs through her messages, all of which we have on the human testimony of the visionaries, almost like a leitmotif. To take some examples:

● "Dear children, you know that it is for your sake I am remaining here so that I may teach you how to make progress on the road of holiness" (1 January 1987).

● "Dear children, if you live the messages, you are living the seeds of holiness" (10 October 1985).

● "Dear children, I desire to lead you on the way of holiness" (9 October 1986).

● "Dear children, from day to day I wish to clothe you in holiness so that you may become more beautiful and more prepared for your Master" (24 October 1985).

Medjugorje's spiritual fruits
The response to Our Lady's call to holiness has been nothing short of sensational. Medjugorje produces spiritual fruit on such a scale

45

that it is a phenomenon of grace and sanctification, a wonder for our times. From this unpretentious source, a mighty crusade of holiness has been launched into every corner of the globe. The holy flames burning in Mary's Immaculate Heart have kindled the hearts of millions of her children the world over.

A leading contributory factor to Medjugorje holiness is the strong Eucharistic devotion that flourishes there and is spread abroad by its multinational visitors. For they are impressed and inspired by the obvious fact that Medjugorje's very heart and hub is the Blessed Sacrament. A myriad offerings of the Saviour's sacrifice are made there, while Holy Communion is distributed to countless numbers. Also, the Blessed Sacrament is the focus of ever-increasing adoration and devotion.

The confessional, too, contributes richly to Medjugorje's sanctifying effects on so many millions of lives. Indeed, Our Lady's strong advocacy of frequent confession is already producing signs here and there of the overall effect she promised – an improvement in the spiritual health of the ailing western Church.

As for Medjugorje-inspired prayer, it has grown to enormous proportions. For the great majority of pilgrims acquire and then take home with them a deep devotion to prayer in general and the Rosary in particular. A further fruit of Medjugorje has been the formation of prayer-groups by the thousand. Bible-reading, too, has received a tremendous fillip. Mention should also be made of the amount of fasting and penance now done by so many in response to the Madonna's appeal.

Medjugorje and youth

It is not least among young people, including those still in their teens, that Medjugorje holiness is spreading fast and far. Especially nowadays, this is a phenomenon in itself: the almost magnetic appeal exerted by Medjugorje over young minds and hearts, and its power to tap those deep reservoirs of idealism, heroism, self-sacrifice and service which are youth's prerogatives.

One thinks here of that exciting and precious quality described by Newman as "a youthful, eager, elastic love and service of

God". It is a quality, he says, that belongs to young people whose faith is active and ardent; but we should all strive to keep it alive and evergreen till the very end of our days.

One thinks here, too, of **Youth 2000** – the Medjugorje-inspired youth movement initiated by a young Englishman, Ernest Williams. Each year it attracts thousands of young people from all over to a week's retreat in Medjugorje during the summer months. What boosts its effectiveness and sanctifying power enormously is that its main focus and inspiration is the Eucharist. **Youth 2000** has now extended its scope to take in the formation of prayer-groups all over the world and to foster within them a special devotion to the Blessed Sacrament.

A youth apostle's testimony

One of the best-known apostles in the English-speaking world, Fr Ken Roberts, has presented Medjugorje with a glowing bouquet. "From one end of the USA to the other," he writes, "I have come across countless young people who are confused, bored, fed-up. They are not at all excited about being Catholics. And they have certainly not got much of a prayer-life. They are turned off the Church. They find Mass dull and meaningless. Many even doubt Our Lord's true presence in the Eucharist.

"I have taken hundreds and hundreds of young people like these to Medjugorje. It's sensational what happens. Within a matter of days they change completely around. They have been to confession. They are now trying to lead pure lives. Mass is now the day's most important event. They spend three or four hours a day in prayer. They do Holy Hours before the Blessed Sacrament. Mary is now their Queen and Mother, and they recite the Rosary every single day. Also, they fast on Wednesdays and Fridays.

"Nor does this transformation last just for a week or two while they are on a spiritual high. Two years later you find they are still persevering in their faith and prayer-life. Quite a few have joined prayer-groups. What is more, one in five of them has started training for the priesthood or has entered religious life."

Medjugorje and priests

Another special category to be powerfully influenced by Medjugorje is priests. Tens of thousands of them have received, as a golden gift from the mother of our Great High Priest, the grace of a fresh spur to be dedicated, holy, prayerful, zealous for souls.

Why Our Lady should have such a predilection for priests is easy to see. To begin with, through the sacrament of Holy Orders, they are closely conformed to the priestly dignity and functions of her son. Secondly, the mother of the Church realises full well the practical wisdom of Vatican II's words: "Priests have the chief part to play in the renovation of Christ's Church." And, to be truly effective as teachers and apostles, such must be their holiness, as Pope St Pius X said, that "they shine like stars in the world". Or as St Bernard put it, "the flame burning within the priest acts as a beacon for his flock".

A high-placed Vatican authority, Cardinal Augustin Mayer, OSB, has testified that Medjugorje's wonderful effect on priests suffices in itself to convince him that the mother of God is at work there in a quite astonishing way. Thus, a well-known British canon lawyer, Fr Lachlan Hughes, SJ, could declare shortly before his death that the pilgrimage he had made to Medjugorje the preceding year was unquestionably the most precious spiritual gift he had received from God since ordination.

To quote Fr Ken Roberts again, this time as spokesman for thousands of priests: "Our Lady of Medjugorje has worked wonders for me. She has renewed my priesthood chiefly by reminding me of why I became a priest and what a priest is. She has renewed the Mass for me and also the hearing of confessions. She has made every individual I talk to or minister to important – as someone who is absolutely unique in God's eyes.

"Yes, Medjugorje is a great place for priests to go to. When they say Mass there and see the church packed with devout faithful, they get a sort of vision or dream of what the priesthood is in itself and of what things back at home could be if they but responded to the great graces which Our Lady gives in Medjugorje. Thus she has re-fired with holiness and revitalised with faith and zeal thou-

sands of her priestly sons, all of whom are key-men in her programme of renewal for the entire Church."

The message spells holiness

But it is to everyone without exception, not just to young people
and priests, that Our Lady addresses her stirring summons to holiness. She has each and every one of her sons and daughters in
mind when she says: "I am your mother, and so I desire to lead
each of you to holiness in all its completeness" (25 May 1987).

To be sanctified, to become truly holy – this is Medjugorje's
bottom line. Holiness sums up the entire Medjugorje package. This
single concept encapsulates Mary's whole five-point message,
Medjugorje's very foundation charter.

For holiness demands in the first place that we renounce our
sinful ways and give the God of the commandments top priority in
our lives. Secondly, holiness works in close harness with faith,
nourishing our minds with its mysteries. As for the third element
of the Medjugorje message – prayer – its whole function is to sustain, promote, deepen holiness.

What is likewise geared to produce these effects on holiness is
the message's fourth component – fasting – which really stands
generally for penance and self-denial, plus the willingness to bear
in our bodies the sufferings of Christ for his mystical body, the
Church (cf. Col 1:24). Fifthly and finally, there is a vital link
between peace and holiness. St James makes this point very clear.
"Peace", he says, "is the seed-ground of holiness, and those who
make peace will win its harvest" (Jm 3:15).

In line with tradition

In exhorting us to be holy and showing us the way, Our Lady of
Medjugorje is not propounding any new-found doctrine or initiat-
ing some fresh and novel approach to spirituality; rather, she is
simply putting before us, in a highly appealing way, the well-tried
truths and practices of Christian tradition.

In other words, the mother of God is replaying, for the benefit
of our spiritually impoverished world, that all-time classic: the

music of the gospel composed by the Holy One of Israel. That is to say, Gospa of Medjugorje is addressing to this benighted age of ours her Son's gospel call to holiness, "Come, follow me." He is inviting us through the lips of his gracious mother, "for I am the way, the truth, and the life...Be ye perfect, as my heavenly Father is perfect...A disciple is no better than his master; he will be fully perfect if he is as his master is" (Lk 7:8; Jn 14:6; Mt 5:48; Mt 10:24).

What the Medjugorje Virgin is also recalling for our benefit is that a Christian, as St Paul and the other New Testament writers took for granted, is "someone called to be holy" (cf. 1 Co 1:2). This was chiefly in consideration of the all-holy, sacred gifts with which the Christian, as such, is endowed. For, at baptism, his entire personality is consecrated to God through sanctifying grace and the indwelling presence of the three divine persons, whereby his human being becomes a flesh-and-blood temple of the Holy Trinity (cf. 1 Co 3:16; Jn 14:23).

Furthermore, the Christian receives at baptism the three theological virtues of faith, hope and charity, plus the seven gifts of the Holy Spirit. Along with this rich supernatural endowment goes the duty, the obligation, binding on every Christian, to be holy like his Lord and Master, reflecting gospel holiness in his every thought, word, action and reaction.

Besides being pure gospel and pure St Paul in content, the Medjugorje Madonna's call to holiness is pure Vatican II. "All Christ's faithful," its document on the modern Church declares, "no matter what their rank or station, have a vocation to the fullness of Christian life and the perfection of charity. All have an invitation, which is binding, to the pursuit of holiness and perfection in their own station of life."

Love, holiness, beauty
In a particularly memorable message, the Queen of Peace said: "You cannot live without holiness. For that reason, you must achieve victory over every sin through love. Overcome every diffi-

culty you encounter in the same way. Dear children, live love within yourselves" (10 July 1986).

Through this living of love within ourselves, we fulfil the first and greatest commandment – the love of God – with our entire heart, mind, soul and strength (cf. Dt 8:5; Mt 22:37). The greater, then, is our love, the deeper is our holiness. Or, as the Imitation of Christ expresses it, "he is truly great who has great charity".

The living equation between love and holiness is glowingly illustrated in the lives of the saints. By loving God with their whole being and doing, they reached the heights of holiness, thus exemplifying Charles de Foucauld's words: "Everything about us, all that we are, should proclaim the gospel from the housetops. Our whole being should be a living witness, a reflection, of Jesus."

An operative word in this context is "whole". Its derivation from the same English root as "holy" indicates that holiness goes hand-in-hand with personal wholeness and psychological completeness, balance, integration and poise. A confirmation of this is again found in the lives of the saints. Precisely because they are holy they are likewise vibrantly whole and well-rounded personalities. As was divinely promised, through losing their lives for God's sake, they find them again (cf. Lk 17:33).

Holiness also produces moral beauty. Pascal referred to it as "the serene, silent beauty of a holy life", a life that is filled with the love of God. Jelena Vasilj, who sees the mother of God interiorly, was moved to ask her (25 March 1985) why she appeared so beautiful. "I am beautiful", came the reply, "because I love. If you want to be beautiful, you, too, must love."

Obstacles on the way

"Dear children," runs the message of 25 July 1987, "I beseech you to take up, beginning today, the way of holiness. I love you and therefore want you to be holy. I do not want Satan to place obstacles in your way."

One obstacle that is apt to set up a formidable roadblock on the way to holiness is fear and hesitation about what this journey will cost us in terms of effort and self-sacrifice. Nor was this human

51

shrinking from the demands of holiness ever expressed more honestly than in the following prayer: "My God", it runs, "I have no strong desire for great holiness. Perhaps I even have a dread of it. But in your mercy, Lord, change me, and give me courage to place no barriers in your way. Holiness frightens me, Lord. You alone can heal me of this false and foolish fear."

For our unheroic selves, it comes as an encouragement to discover that the author of this prayer was St Claude de la Colombière, spiritual director of St Margaret Mary. Nor is he the only one of heaven's citizens to have been human enough to experience such things. Francis of Assisi, for one, did exactly the same.

Another roadblock Satan places in our way when possible is discouragement, especially after a fall. There is only one way of dismantling this roadblock. We must, without delay, say sorry to God for having sinned and then resume our service of him with greater fervour than ever. That is, the unhorsed warrior must simply pick himself up, re-mount, and re-enter the fray.

Undoubtedly, it is to the vast majority of people that St Anthony of the Desert's dictum applies: "The spiritual life is a long series of fresh beginnings." One of the most celebrated of fresh beginnings was that staged by the Apostle Peter. Overcoming his discouragement and worse with a humble act of contrition after his fall, for that very reason he rose a holier man than before and therefore, too, became all the more effective as an Apostle.

Keep on going on
A further roadblock Satan loves to erect on the road of holiness is referred to by St Paul as "weariness in well-doing" (Ga 6:9; 2 Th 3:13). What he means is that first fervour tends to wane and enthusiasm to wear away. The worst cases can end up in total burn-out; or, to quote another Pauline phrase, "they make a shipwreck of the faith" (1 Tm 1:19).

The remedy for this is patience, constancy and faithfulness. The Virgin Most Faithful touched upon this in a specific message given through Jelena (8 December 1983): "Be persevering and tenacious." By taking one day at a time, ever endeavouring, as Bishop

Challoner put it, "to do ordinary things extraordinarily well", let us remain tireless in well-doing till life's journey is over.

Scripture provides us with an apt exhortation in this regard: "Our longing is to see you all showing the same eagerness right up to the end, looking forward to the fulfilment of your hope; listless no more, but followers of all those whose faith and patience are to bring them into possession of the good things promised them" (Heb 1:11-12).

Mobilising the Church Militant

The whole point about Medjugorje is that the Queen of Prophets is rousing and mobilising the Church Militant, stirring it into prayer, vigilance and action. Throughout the ranks of the Christian militia, Mary's voice is ringing like a reveille. The message she proclaims is a call to arms, a battle-cry, in our warfare against God's enemies and ours – our fallen human nature, this fallen world, and the fallen angels.

Nobody can deny that Medjugorje's stirring stimulus is badly needed. As Our Lady makes clear, a crisis situation prevails in wide areas of the Church. God is seriously neglected and his commandments flouted. Prayer plays little part in many lives; and, in a large number of hearts and homes, faith is dying of attrition.

So the trumpet-call sounding from Medjugorje is timely and providential. So low are general standards in the Church that mediocrity abounds. Few of us are anywhere near being Christian soldiers of the calibre envisaged by St Paul. Perhaps more fitting would be St Bernard's label: "Pampered soldiers of a thorn-crowned King".

To this King and Commander, we all have reason to address Amy Carmichael's prayer: "From silken self, O Captain, free thy soldier who would follow thee. Let me not sink to be a clod. Make me thy fuel, O Flame of God."

Closing prayer to Gospa

O *sinless mother of God, pray for us, your sinful children, that we may become truly holy after the pattern you have taught us at Medjugorje. May the world-wide crusade of holiness you have started there spread to more and more hearts, kindling in them the fire that burns in the Sacred Heart of your Son and in your own Immaculate Heart.*

Increase within us, all-holy mother Mary, the spirit of prayer and a deep devotion to the mysteries of the Eucharist. May we be strengthened to accept our crosses cheerfully and to unite our sufferings with those of Jesus for the conversion of sinners.

O full-of-grace Gospa, protect and prosper all the graces of sanctification you have gained for us in and through Medjugorje.

Continue to inspire in young hearts an ardent desire for prayer, purity, sacrifice and service. And may they provide tomorrow's Church with holy priests and religious to carry on its work. Endow today's priests and religious with the gift of prayerfulness and a burning zeal for the kingdom of holiness.

Bless, O sinless Gospa, the crusade of Medjugorje holiness you have launched into our world. Make us into valiant and ardent Krizevac Crusaders, consecrated to your Son's cross and consumed with zeal for his cause and his kingdom.

4

The World's Confessional

"Mary, the refuge of sinners, awakens in us the need to be holy. Her sanctuaries are places of conversion, penance and reconciliation." When Pope John Paul II spoke these words in 1979, he little realised how literally and richly they were to be exemplified just two years later in a Croatian village destined to become world-famous as a Marian sanctuary. For Medjugorje is strongly, indeed characteristically, a place of conversion and penance. As for reconciliation, the sacrament bearing this name enjoys there the highest of profiles.

So much so, that Fr René Laurentin writes of Medjugorje: "It is that place where more confessions are heard than anywhere else in the world, as many as 150 confessors being kept busy on some days. Moreover, you also find there the highest proportion of 'conversion' confessions – such as bring about a reform of lives sunk in materialism and perversion, the reconciliation of spouses, not to mention other kinds of spiritual fruit."

A bishop testifies

Any confessor who has actually heard confessions in Medjugorje would confirm this. For example, an Irish bishop, Seamus Hegarty of Raphoe, is on record as saying: "My most outstanding experience in Medjugorje was the hearing of confessions. One day I spent three hours doing so. And I am sure that, during that time, I heard more confessions of the kind that are basic and come from the depths of the heart than during all the twenty-one years of my priesthood. I could not help being moved by the clear workings of grace in the quality of the confessions I heard."

Medjugorje has surely brought about much joy before the angels of God over so many sinners receiving the sacrament of penance – and continuing to do so on a regular basis.

Our Lady promotes it

A major reason why the Sacrament of Reconciliation features so prominently in Medjugorje is that, right from the outset, Our Lady has not only recommended but insisted that we have recourse to it at least once a month. And by "we" she means literally every single member of the Church in the West – that is, the Roman Catholic communion.

To quote her words as communicated to us through her human mouthpiece, Marija: "One must invite people to go to confession each month, especially the first Saturday...Monthly confession will be a remedy for the Church in the West. One must convey this message to the West" (6 August 1981)..."I am happy because you have begun to prepare the monthly observance of the Sacrament of Reconciliation. That will be good for the whole world" (1 October 1982).

We have here the clearest indication that she who is the Refuge of Sinners prizes this sacrament as a precious gift from heaven. To quote Newman on the subject: "If there is a heavenly idea in the Catholic Church, then surely, next after the Blessed Sacrament, it is confession." The reason is that it reaches down into the deeps of divine compassion and human sinfulness alike. "It is the sacrament", Pope John Paul II points out, "where God's mercy meets man's misery."

Confession's origins take us back to the wounded Christ of Good Friday, from whose pierced side flowed blood and water: blood symbolic of the Eucharist; and water signifiying our cleansing from original sin through baptism, and from post-baptismal sins through penance. Equally, this sacrament takes us back to the Risen Saviour empowering his apostles on Easter Sunday to bestow his pardoning grace on contrite sinners through the remission of their guilt.

Confession counters sin

It is because the sinless Mary is calling us to holiness, deep holiness, that she so zealously advocates frequent confession. For holiness fundamentally means turning away from sin and towards

God. And this is precisely what confession has in mind, besides fortifying us with the sacramental grace of fresh beginnings. Or as St Francis of Sales puts it: "Confession is not meant only as a sponge which rubs out but a tonic which strengthens."

Sins are traditionally labelled mortal or venial according as they are grave or otherwise. St John was referring to the former when he said that "there is a sin which kills" (1 Jn 5:16). What it kills within the soul is supernatural life. In other words, mortal sin is grace's graveyard; accordingly a "confession of obligation" is called for in such a situation. As writers of the early Church used to say, the life-raft of sacramental penance is required by those who have incurred spiritual shipwreck through mortal sin.

It is so-called "confessions of devotion" that Our Lady of Medjugorje has principally in mind when she advocates that everyone should approach the sacrament at least once a month. Such confessions imply venial sins only. Yet we should never allow ourselves to become careless or cavalier in their regard. Venial though they may be, sins of this kind are none the less offences against the all-holy God of the commandments, and were instrumental in inflicting additional pain on the suffering Redeemer during his bitter Passion.

Therefore, venial sins are evil, hateful and displeasing to God. Among their other consequences, they lead to mortal sin; they dim the soul's beauty and diminish fervour; they weaken faith and choke the avenues of grace; they dull the conscience and incur temporal punishment.

Light in darkness
Nobody is free from venial sins. On one occasion, St Gertrude, in preparing herself for confession, experienced difficulty in recalling any blemishes on her conscience. Suddenly a ray of sunshine shot through the room, revealing multiple tiny particles of dust which were not apparent in the ordinary light. The saint saw herein a sign that the light of the Holy Spirit shining into human consciences will unfailingly reveal all imperfections to those with eyes to see.

In a locution to Jelena, the Virgin Mary, having recommended

57

her to go to confession regularly, added: "Confession should give an impulse to your faith. It should stimulate you and bring you closer to Jesus" (7 November 1983). Jelena admitted to feeling very confused and embarrassed at first over this recommendation, since she felt she had nothing to say in confession. But before long, she began to see her faults all-too-clearly in the light of her ever-growing union with the God of holiness and forgiveness.

Keys of the Kingdom

In fostering frequent confession, the Mother of the Church is endorsing, as she does in many another context, what the Church's official magisterium has told us time and time again. Vatican II, for example, expressly commended frequent Holy Communion and confession, at the same time appealing to priests to make themselves available as confessors on all reasonable occasions. For in this sublime sacrament there takes place, to quote Pope John Paul II, "a personal encounter of the sinner with Christ".

This phrase pinpoints the dual agency that operates in the Sacrament of Reconciliation – the compassionate Christ and the penitent sinner. So overwhelming is the divine compassion, says the Curé d'Ars, that "God is swifter to forgive a repentant sinner than is a mother to snatch her child from the danger of fire."

Acting in the person of Christ is the minister of this sacrament – an ordained priest. And, in approaching the sacrament, the penitent is having recourse to what St Augustine terms "the keys of the Church", in whose person, too, and armed with whose delegation and jurisdiction, the priest exercises his ministerial role. Through the judicial act pronounced by the priest in the confessional, the penitent's sins are forgiven or retained, as the case may be (Mt 16:19; Jn 20:23). What is certain is that the words of absolution spoken by the priest contribute the principal efficacy to the sacrament.

The keys to yourself

But priestly absolution remains abortive without the penitent's contribution to the dynamics of confession. This contribution depends on three all-important keys to which the penitent alone has access. For they open doors to his private world of self, his inviolable kingdom of conscience and free will. In other words, the repentant sinner must contribute three essential constituents for the sacrament to be valid: contrition for his sins, their due avowal, and a purpose of amendment.

First, having examined the intimate privacies within his conscience known only to God and himself, the penitent must, as it were, unlock his heart in order to release sentiments of true sorrow for sin.

Next, he must equivalently apply the key to his own tongue, unloosing it to reveal, to bare, his transgressions – sins of commission and omission. The sole obligation here is that he must specify the nature and number of any mortal sins committed since his last confession. This self-accusation before what is surely the frankest and most sincere tribunal in the world further acts as a therapy, a release value for pent-up guilt, anxiety and remorse. As Paul Bourget has said, the most noxious poison known to the human heart is silence.

The third key requiring to be applied by the penitent is that which opens his will to accept and implement, humbly and readily, whatever penance is prescribed by the confessor; also, the resolve to avoid all sin and its occasions in future.

The fruits of confession

So rich and varied are these that we cannot wonder at the Medjugorje Madonna's great zeal for frequent confession. Its primary effect, of course, is in the order of sanctifying grace, which it restores to a penitent making a confession of obligation, while simply increasing it in a confession of devotion.

In addition, confessional grace deletes the guilt of sin, also remitting the temporal punishment due on it in a more efficacious way specific to the sacrament. Furthermore, it increases our love of God and helps to heal sin's harmful effects in the soul.

The Council of Trent lists among the sacramental benefits "peace and serenity of conscience", adding that these are frequently accompanied by "overpowering spiritual consolation". Besides this, confession restores a penitent's self-respect and self-confidence.

Again to quote Pope John Paul II: "By this sacrament we are renewed in fervour, strengthened in our resolve, and buoyed by divine encouragement. The personal encounter with the forgiving Jesus is a divine means which keeps alive in our hearts and in our communities a consciousness of sin in its perennial and tragic reality, and increases holiness."

Among the Sacrament of Reconciliation's further effects is that it invigorates our weak wills and does much to banish discouragement and depression. Equally, it acts like a tonic on our weariness in well-doing, our coldness towards God and his service, our tepidity, complacency, lethargy, frailty and fickleness, our ever-present proclivity towards sin and its occasions.

Pope Paul VI laid special emphasis on that effect of confession which is for St Thomas the sacrament's principal pastoral function – it prepares us to receive the Eucharist more worthily. And the pontiff went on to say: "Frequent confession remains a privileged source of blessing, holiness, peace and joy."

The mind of the Holy See

In prompting us to go frequently to confession, Our Lady is simply directing our attention to what the Church has long been saying. Ever since Pope St Pius X, whose aim was to reverse the Jansenist trend against early and also frequent confession, a whole succession of popes have raised their voices in support of this cause.

Pius XII declared that frequent confession had been introduced into practice under the direct inspiration of the Holy Spirit. And both Paul VI and John Paul II in turn explicitly endorsed this view. Pius XII warned the younger clergy not to make light of this great sacrament nor to lessen esteem for its frequent reception. Such attitudes, he added, were disastrous for the mystical body of the Church, displeasing to the Holy Spirit, and dangerous for the spiritual life. The pontiff appealed to priests themselves to receive confession with frequency and devotion.

Because this practice "ensures more rapid progress day by day in the path of virtue," Pius XII continued, "confession should be received frequently even by those who are conscious only of venial sins. For by this means we grow in a true knowledge of ourselves and in Christian humility; bad habits are uprooted; spiritual negligence and apathy are prevented; the conscience is purified and the will strengthened; salutary spiritual direction is obtained; and grace is increased by the efficacy of the sacrament."

Two more popes

Pope Paul VI, in declaring 1975 a Holy Year, invited all Catholics "to discover the meaning and practice of frequent confession". The ready availability of priests for this purpose, he pointed out, tends of itself to act as an occasion of grace by encouraging the faithful to confess their sins on a regular basis.

As for John Paul II, in his Apostolic Exhortation on confession, he, too, urged priests to make the sacrament easily accessible to those desirous of receiving it, besides becoming regular recipients themselves. He addressed the same appeal to the entire German hierarchy, asking them to do everything they could to lead both priests and people back to a true esteem for private confession at frequent intervals.

Nor has any German bishop responded to that appeal more concretely, or in a more original way, than Karl Braun of Eichstätt. In his 1991 Lenten pastoral, he warmly encouraged his faithful to embark regularly on what he called "that most effective of all peace-marches" – the march that leads penitents to God's sacramental peace in the confessional.

Somebody who made that sacramental peace-march faithfully every week of his life was Pope John XXIII, as he narrated in his diary when he was eighty years old.

Confession in serious decline

The mother of Christ is urgently drawing our attention to the sad truth that the Church's official directives in this matter have been seriously neglected. Consequently, recourse to the Sacrament of Reconciliation in private confession, despite so many papal voices raised in its favour, has fallen into a state of virtual disuse. Furthermore, besides an appalling ignorance, a widespread lack of discipline prevails about the subject.

Thus the practice of going to confession is at a very low ebb in many a parish nowadays. As it is, penitents are for the most part elderly or middle-aged – the product of a previous and more enlightened pastoral formation. If and when young people can be persuaded to make their confession, the priest is apt to discover that they are wholly unfamiliar with practical procedures in that sacred tribunal. What is still more worrying, they are often vague and worse regarding the difference between mortal and venial sins. In many instances, too, they know next to nothing even about the act of contrition.

A further disturbing factor is that a good many people go on receiving Holy Communion even when mortal sins committed since their last confession remain unconfessed. They do so under the misapprehension that an act of contrition suffices for this purpose.

In his Apostolic Exhortation devoted to the Sacrament of Penance, Pope John Paul II strongly condemned these and other false practices. He also reminded us of the grave duty of confessing mortal sins privately after having received general absolution in their regard.

Medjugorje's main task

But this disarray concerning confession is far from being an isolated feature of today's Church. Rather, it reflects the general *malaise* throughout the entire body. Our Lady is acutely concerned about this, telling the visionaries that faith is growing weaker and weaker in some regions; prayer is neglected, God is to a great extent treated like an outsider; sin has lost much of its meaning, and the divine commandments are being flouted on an ever-increasing scale.

The Queen of Peace summed it up by stating that the whole Western Church is in a sick and weak condition. And the medicine, the antidote, she prescribes for her Son's ailing mystical body is monthly confession by its every member. Through this means, she assures us, whole regions of the Church will be healed.

So what Immaculate Mary is here equivalently saying is that regular confession, far from being simply one item among many in her Medjugorje package, is, pastorally speaking, its key component, a war-winning weapon she is placing in the hands of the hard-pressed Church Militant.

It can reasonably be maintained, then, that the Church's crying need for the medicine of monthly confession actually constitutes the main reason, the principal motivation, behind Mary's dramatic intervention in Medjugorje.

What we learn from Church history, Karl Rahner explains, is that it is always some pressing need, if not an actual crisis situation, which prompts the Queen of Prophets to resort to private revelation as a providential means of dealing with it, once the Church's ordinary means are seen to be unavailing in the circumstances.

The ordinary means at the Church's disposal, as we saw earlier, were repeatedly urged by a succession of popes, and echoed by Vatican II, in their support of frequent confession. But their voices, alas, went unheeded – and the current sorry situation has ensued.

Confession and the Medjugorje message

Why frequent confession is so commended by the Queen of Peace can be clearly seen in the close identity between the sacrament's key elements and the five main points of the message.

In the first place, the sacrament designed to deal with what Newman calls "the weakness and waywardness of the human heart" directs us away from wrongdoing and towards him who pardons. Secondly, faith plays a leading role in the confessional – faith in the God of forgiveness, faith in the power of God operating through his ordained delegate duly armed with the Church's jurisdiction, faith in the inflow of sacramental grace.

The Medjugorje message's third component – prayer – also enters into the dynamics of confession under the forms of contrition, thanksgiving and expiation. As for penance – the fourth component – it lends its very name to the sacrament, so integral is it both as the virtue of penance (that is, penitence, repentance) and in its other role as the acceptance and performance of whatever reparation is imposed by the confessor.

Finally, peace, which is the fifth and crowning element of Mary's Medjugorje message, flows copiously through the Sacrament of Reconciliation – peace of conscience, peace with him who forgives us our trespasses, peace with the Church, against which, too, because of the Communion of Saints binding us all together, our sins have offended.

Closing prayer to Gospa

We thank you, Gospa *of Medjugorje, for the inspiration and spur you are giving us to resort frequently to your Son's sacrament of pardon and peace. Help us to prize it as a precious source of grace and sanctification, and as a powerful stimulus and support in our daily efforts to model our lives on your Medjugorje message.*

Through your powerful intercession, O Mother of the Church, may it be healed and helped, as you assure us it will, through the agency of this sacramental medicine.

Mother of our Great High Priest, bless all priests with a holy zeal both for confessing their own sins regularly and for hearing the confessions of those wishing to approach this sacred tribunal.

May we all share, O Queen of the Angels, in the joy there is before the celestial spirits over those many sinners, ourselves included, who, thanks to the gracious prompting you provide in Medjugorje, benefit regularly by the blessings of the Sacrament of Penance.

5

Stronghold of the Eucharist

In speaking about the Eucharist, we touch the very heart of the matter – the Medjugorje matter. The mother of Christ plays a prominent role there, to be sure. But Medjugorje is not primarily about Mary, nor even mainly about her. Its principal focus is rather upon the fruit of her womb – the Word Incarnate, Emmanuel-made-Eucharist. And in Medjugorje Our Lady performs the identical subsidiary role she has traditionally played elsewhere down the generations, the role of the Lord's handmaid, prophet, signpost.

So everything the Medjugorje Madonna says and does is simply pointing us towards her tabernacled Son and proclaiming his gospel. Thus her basic message is nothing but an echo, faithful, eloquent, contemporary and urgent, of that gospel. And towards the living of her message, as she knows best of all, the Eucharist is to a unique degree inspiring and tonic. For her message is essentially a call to holiness. And the Church leaves us in no doubt as to where holiness is to be found. "Lord God," runs one of her liturgical prayers, "make us truly holy by the Eucharist, which you give us as the source of all holiness" (Offertory Prayer, Feast of St Ignatius, 31 July).

A three-sided mystery
In line with traditional teaching, Vatican II emphasised the unique importance of the Eucharist, recognising in it "the entire wealth of the Church and the source whence flows the grace of all the sacraments".

The Eucharistic mystery presents us with three different aspects. First of all, there is Christ's true presence. He who is the Church's founder, the fountainhead of all graces, the author of our faith and of all the sacraments, is actually, factually, truly present, complete

65

both as to his divinity and glorified humanity. Newman never got over the glad surprise, on becoming a Catholic, of finding in our churches what he called "a treasure unutterable" – the abiding presence of the Word Incarnate. Our Lady made this same point in one of her messages: "Churches merit respect and are set apart as holy because God, who became Man, dwells in them day and night" (25 April 1988).

In the second place, the Eucharistic sacrament presents us in the Mass with the mystery of the Lord's sacrificial death. This takes place when the bread and wine are separately consecrated into the body and blood of him who, in this sacramental action as in the Good Friday sacrifice it represents, is both priest and victim.

With good reason, then, the mother of God could instruct the visionaries: "The Mass is the greatest of all prayers. You will never be able to grasp its grandeur" (15 May 1983). St John Vianney used to say that, if we could truly appreciate the Mass for what it is, "we would die of love and gratitude".

The third aspect of the Eucharistic mystery is that it brings us the Lord's true presence as Holy Communion – that is, as living bread, spiritual food, viaticum on the long pilgrimage of life.

Moreover, the Blessed Sacrament's continuous presence in our tabernacles is a standing invitation for us to adore the Lord and enter into close spiritual communion with him, thus enriching ourselves with the treasures that are his to give.

The mother of the Eucharistic Jesus is greatly pleased when we do this. "Thank you for adoring my Son in the Sacred Host," she once said to the locutionary Jelena after making a Holy Hour. "That touches me very much" (26 January 1984). And this recalls the gentle appeal she made to the Garabandal visionary. "Conchita," she said, "why do you not go more often to visit my Son in the tabernacle? He is waiting for you there, night and day."

But the Medjugorje Virgin, in addition to stirring our devotion to the Eucharistic mysteries, bids us "enter as deeply as we can" into a true understanding of them (1 June 1984). So, with this in view, let us look in turn at the three aspects of the sacrament we have just been considering.

The Master is present

As truly as he was in Bethany, the Master is present in our tabernacles and calls us to unite ourselves with him through faith and love. His presence here takes the sacramental form of a circular wheaten wafer, a frail white disc of unleavened bread that, having been transubstantiated through the consecratory words spoken by a priest, now has the identity and life of the new being it has become – Jesus, mighty God, Son of the Virgin Mary. In St Robert Southwell's words, "the God of hosts in slender host doth dwell".

Of course, neither sense nor reason can perceive the Lord's presence in the Blessed Sacrament. Faith alone avails for that. We can see why, as the visionaries tell us, Our Lady so prizes this virtue, which attains its very Everest in the Eucharist. Indeed, we honour this sacrament as the mystery of faith, the mystery that outfaiths all others, since here is found faith's very author as well as its eventual consummator.

Though based entirely on revelation taught us by the infallible Church, faith can draw support from reason in dealing with this mystery. "A God who became Man", said Chesterton, "should have no difficulty in becoming Bread." Newman points out that "transubstantiation is difficult, impossible to imagine. But how", he goes on, "is it difficult to believe?"

The soft glow of the sanctuary lamp signals the presence of him who is the light of his mother's life and the love of her heart. No wonder, then, that she again and again tells us to approach the tabernacle with great frequency, faith and confidence. She equivalently says with St John Vianney: "Everything's there, my children!" Or in St Peter Eymard's words: "Treat the Blessed Sacrament as a living Person!"

Eucharistic adoration

Strong emphasis is laid by the Lord's mother on Eucharistic adoration. We have already noted how she specially thanked Jelena for spending some time before the Blessed Sacrament. On another occasion, she expressed great pleasure at seeing the girl stay for the Holy Hour after Mass one Thursday evening, adding that this devotion was "very beautiful" (28 May 1983). Our Lady has also recommended prayer-groups to spend as much time as possible in the presence of her Eucharistic Son.

In fostering devotion to the Blessed Sacrament, the Mother of the Church is simply endorsing what several recent popes have said. Paul VI, for example, counselled everyone to visit the tabernacled Lord every day, if possible. As for John Paul II, he declared, on the occasion of his inaugurating daily exposition of the Blessed Sacrament in St Peter's Basilica in 1981: "The Church and the world have great need of Eucharistic devotion. Jesus waits for us in this sacrament of love. Let us be generous with our time in going to meet him, ready to make reparation for the evils of the world."

The Queen of Peace invites us to place ourselves with all possible frequency in the presence of the living, loving Bread of Heaven, cultivating an intimate personal relationship with him. Indeed, this is the main reason for Our Lord's being there in the first place. "The Eucharist", to quote Pope John Paul II once again, "brings us close to God in a stupendous way. It is the sacrament of his closeness to man."

As an added incentive, the Church has attached a plenary indulgence (subject to the usual conditions) to our saying five decades of the Rosary, or spending at least half-an-hour before the Blessed Sacrament.

The practice of spending a full hour in that holy presence, which enjoys much popularity in Medjugorje, is catching on fast among pilgrims from all parts of the world. "Could you not watch one hour with me?" Reparation for sin, in union with the Christ of Gethsemane, is a key feature of this devotion; it affords an ideal opportunity for prayer on behalf of sinners and unbelievers, towards whom the visionary Mirjana, in particular, taught by Our Lady, feels such tender compassion.

Eucharistic developments
One of the most exciting and significant Eucharistic developments from Medjugorje is **Youth 2000**. This is an international move-

ment which, ever since 1989, has brought thousands of young people to Medjugorje each summer for a week-long festival of prayer, mostly centred upon the Blessed Sacrament.

A further Medjugorje-inspired development, closely identified with **Youth 2000**, is the formation among young people all over the world of prayer-groups devoted to Eucharistic adoration. It is hoped that this will increasingly tie in with and fuel another Eucharistic development that is gaining much added impetus and momentum from Medjugorje – Perpetual Adoration of the Blessed Sacrament in parish churches.

Outside the Mass, this is surely the crown, the supreme form, of Eucharistic adoration, bringing untold blessings not only upon the parishes in question but upon the entire world. Cardinal Gagnon acknowledges that he owes his priestly vocation to the fact that he lived in a parish where Perpetual Adoration was practised. And Mother Teresa is on record as saying: "Perpetual Adoration is one of the most beautiful things you could ever think of doing. People are hungry for God."

The sacrifice of the Mass
We now turn to the second aspect of the Eucharistic mystery: the true presence not only of the Risen Lord but of his redeeming sacrifice on Good Friday. In other words, the offerer and victim of that sacrifice re-enacts and thus reproduces on the altar, in a real, albeit sacramental manner, the selfsame sacrifice he offered on the cross.

What brings about this amazing repeat-performance of the Lord's Golgotha sacrifice is the formula of consecration pronounced by the priest over the bread and wine. These elements become transubstantiated into Christ's body and blood, their separate consecration serving both to signify and effect, in the sacramental order of things, their real-life separation which took place on Golgotha. Thus, the Sacrifice of the Mass is identical in substance with the bloodstained one witnessed by the Priest-Victim's mother standing at the foot of that austere, perpendicular altar which was the cross.

So nobody could possibly understand better than she, the mother of the Eucharist, the full import of St Paul's words: "Each time you break this bread and drink this cup, you show forth the death of the Lord until he comes again" (1 Co 11:26).

Mary stresses the Mass

This is why the central role and importance of Mass is given such prominence by the Lord's mother. In a wide range of messages communicated variously through the visionaries and Jelena, she instructs us to value Mass as "the centre of our lives and the highest form of prayer" (March 1983). She extols its "grandeur and beauty" (3 April 1986). We should cherish Mass as being, in its unique way, "an experience of God" (16 May 1985). It is her wish that the Mass becomes for us "the day's supreme gift, the treasures of which are inexhaustible, because Jesus gives us there such plentiful graces" (30 March 1984). It is her further wish that we "look forward joyously" to Mass, and that we attend it "with active participation and with love in our hearts" (3 April 1986; 11 January 1982).

As an added incentive for us to assist at Mass daily, whenever possible, the mother of the Eucharist invites us to "show our love for her" by doing so, assuring us again that her Son will reward us abundantly (21 November 1985). Small children, she says, should also be brought (7 March 1985). Her overriding desire is that we should "live the Mass" (25 April 1988). In other words, we must make it "a conscious part of our lives" (3 April 1986).

Through the lens of faith

The Eucharistic mysteries being so exalted and enriching, we can see why Our Lady so wants us to enter as deeply as we can, through faith aided by reason, into their meaning. Thereby, we shall grow to love these mysteries more and more and live them all the better.

The genius of this great sacrament, which is with good reason styled "blessed," is that it enables the Word Incarnate to transcend the limitations of time and space, and to re-offer, on behalf of our sinful selves, his Good Friday sacrificial death. We, in turn, also thanks to this great sacrament, are enabled to contemplate, through the telescopic lens of faith, that which is here represented in ritual form: the blood-drenched actualities of the Saviour's crucifixion and death.

In and through the Mass, and again deploying faith's powerful lens, we are further enabled to contemplate the Christ of Holy Thursday as he institutes the sacrament of his love in that lamp-lit supper-room; and, too, as he offers, in anticipation and advance, the selfsame sacrifice he would make the following afternoon on Calvary and, in the centuries to come, upon a myriad altars throughout the world.

These considerations prompted Newman to say: "Nothing is so consoling, so piercing, so thrilling, so overcoming, as the Mass. It is not a mere form of words. It is a great action, the greatest action that can be on earth."

Mass in Medjugorje

At a very early stage in the Medjugorje story (the eighth day, in fact), the Queen of Peace so guided events and circumstances that her daily apparition to the visionaries became integrated into the evening liturgy consisting of the public Rosary followed by Mass. As a happy result, the evening liturgy has become the main item in Medjugorje's daily programme. The visionary Marija once indicated how right her priorities are when she stated that, if ever she were faced with a choice between having an apparition and attending Mass, she would opt for the latter.

Medjugorje has already become a Eucharistic giant on account of the many Masses celebrated there by tens of thousands of priest pilgrims. There is a concelebrated Mass for each of the major language-groups at an appointed time in the forenoon. The Mass for English-speakers (normally at 10 o'clock) can muster anything up to thirty or forty concelebrants.

But it is the evening liturgy that forms the highlight of each day's programme. The twin-towered church is jam-packed, down to its last cubic inch, with a huge overflow crowd gathered all around outside. When the weather is good, the new outdoor pavilion with its domed roof is used as a sanctuary, the massive congregation spreading itself on all sides around it.

Certainly that evening liturgy is unique, overwhelming, unforgettable. There is a wonderful atmosphere of faith and devotion among the massive congregation. And its multi-national, multi-lingual composition makes it into a microcosm of the universal Church. You sense vividly there that the Eucharist is truly the symbol of Church unity, the Bread that sanctifies and feeds the one Body of Christ.

Another long-lingering memory is of the congregational hymn-singing during this liturgy; it is as spirited and devotional as you will have heard for a long time. Honourable mention should also be made of that brave little harmonium wheezing its accompaniment to the melodies – those haunting melodies that grace so many of the slow, Slav hymns.

For the concelebrants at that main evening Mass, of whom there can be anything up to 150, it is an unforgettable experience to look out on the sea of faces and to sense the atmosphere of faith and fervour.

Another moving experience is to take part, along with dozens of other priests, in distributing Holy Communion to those multitudes. As you pass down long lines of communicants awaiting you in the open air – the soft air of evening – you see gorgeous sunset patterns against the sky, silhouetting the western hills sharply against the skyline.

The Bread of Life

We now come to the third aspect of the Eucharistic sacrament, namely, its function as food for our souls: Holy Communion. Incidentally, there are staggering statistics on the total number of hosts distributed during the first ten years in Medjugorje; a conservative estimate puts it at at least twenty million.

A significant number of these communicants are young people. Newman's words come to mind in this context. "It is the boast of the Catholic religion," he says, "that it has the gift of making the young heart chaste; and why is this but that it gives us Jesus for our food and Mary for our nursing-mother."

Our heavenly nursing-mother strongly commends frequent communion, also advocating regular confession – the sacrament specifically designed, St Thomas teaches, to prepare us for a worthier reception of the Eucharist.

Holy Communion is essentially spiritual nourishment, the Bread of Life. "When the priest presents the host and shows it to you," the Curé d'Ars once declared, "you can say: 'There is my food!'"

Being food, Holy Communion sustains, nourishes, builds up our spiritual life by bringing us growth in grace. And, in the process, it fortifies us against human frailty and the dangers posed by diabolical temptations. St John Chrysostom wrote in this regard: "Let us go away from that table as so many lions breathing out fire – fire that is terrible in the devil's sight!"

Another effect of Holy Communion is that it provides a pledge, a guarantee, of our own bodily resurrection. He who is the Resurrection and the Life expressly linked this great promise to our reception of his body in the Eucharist (cf. Jn 6:40). What is more, his presence in the Blessed Sacrament as the Risen Saviour also serves as the pattern of our own bodily resurrection (cf. Ph 3:21).

Mother of the Eucharist

Vatican II, in speaking of "the close and indissoluble union between Jesus and Mary", concluded that "this must also apply to Jesus in the Blessed Sacrament".

It must indeed. Mary enjoys unbrokenly the Beatific Vision; therefore, she is in the presence of her Eucharistic Son – and, no less, of the Father and the Holy Spirit, inasmuch as the three Divine Persons are inseparably linked in the unity of their identical being and substance. Equally present with Mary in the hallowed ambience of the tabernacle are all her co-participants in the vision of God's glory – the angels and the saints.

So the Queen of Heaven and the entire heavenly court are ever close to the tabernacled presence of Christ. "Dear children," runs an early message, "adore the most Blessed Sacrament of the Altar unceasingly. I am always present when the faithful are there in adoration. Special graces are received at those times" (15 March 1984).

No wonder, then, that the Queen of Peace aims to make all Medjugorje roads lead to the tabernacle as to its heart and hub.

Eucharist and message

The links between them are very close. For a start, Our Lady's message simply re-formulates what her Eucharistic Son proclaimed in his gospel. Furthermore, he now embodies and lives her message in and through the Blessed Sacrament. For there he offers to the Father not only supreme worship but sacrifice for our sins. And, as author of our faith, he enables us to apprehend these mysteries in the first place and, in so far as we can, comprehend them as well. Prayer is continuously offered by the head of the mystical body for all his members. As for reparation for sin and peace with God, these are achieved through the blood of his cross, re-shed each time the consecratory words are spoken at the altar.

Above all, our efforts to practise Our Lady's message are greatly enlightened and fortified through the Blessed Sacrament. For in the Mass we co-offer with him to the Father supreme praise, besides sorrow for our sins. Our faith is toned up by this contract with what is the mystery of faith par excellence.

The same benefit applies to our prayer-life in general. Also, we receive a fresh incentive to be generous in practising penance; that is, in bearing in our bodies the mortifications of Jesus so that his life may be made manifest in us (cf. 2 Co 4:10). Finally, the Eucharist unites us with the Prince of Peace himself, abidingly present in his great sacrament of peace.

Croatian Bethlehem

In Medjugorje, scene of a myriad Masses, communions by the million, and much Eucharistic adoration, multitudes of pilgrims are being led to Jesus through Mary. This outwardly insignificant village nestling among its familiar hills bears close comparison with another situated amid the austere hills of Judaea – the village of Bethlehem, which means literally, "house of bread".

Medjugorje is likewise a Bethlehem, a house of bread – the Bread of Life, the Bread that is Eucharist. And to this latter-day Bethlehem come throngs of wise men and women, led thereto from all directions by the star of faith. Like their biblical counterparts, they find the radiant young mother with her Child – now wrapped in the swaddling clothes of the Eucharist and laid in that manger which is the tabernacle.

First, they venerate the holy young mother. Then, kneeling, they worship the Child and offer him their gifts – the fivefold gift prescribed by the Medjugorje Madonna: loyalty to God and avoidance of sin; faith in God teaching us through his Church; faithfulness to prayer; generosity in doing penance and making reparation for sin; peace and reconciliation with God and our neighbour.

Closing prayer to Gospa

We thank you, all-holy mother of the Eucharist, for the radiant light Medjugorje is shedding on these sacred mysteries, and for your warm and zealous encouragement in their regard. Stir within us a deep, tender devotion to your Son ever-present behind the tabernacle veil.

Win for us the grace, Gospa of Medjugorje, to make Mass and Holy Communion more and more into the centrepiece of our daily lives. And win for us the further grace, O sinless and beautiful Mother Mary, to be generous in practising Eucharistic adoration, including the Holy Hour in reparation for the sins of the world. We also ask you to pray that Medjugorje may inspire the spread of Perpetual Adoration of the Blessed Sacrament to many other parishes across the world.

O Gospa of the Blessed Sacrament, strengthen us to persevere until death in the grace and peace of your Divine Son, and so merit eternal life and the resurrection of our bodies, of which his glorified humanity in the Eucharist is prototype, promise and pledge.

6

We Walk with Angels

On 7 May 1985 the visionary Ivanka had her final regular apparition; in her account of it, she wrote: "I have never seen Mary quite as beautiful – so very gentle and beautiful – as she was this evening. And her gown, which, like her veil and crown, was covered with gold and silver sequins of light, was the loveliest I have ever seen in my life. With Our Lady were two angels, likewise dressed in gold and silver garments. So beautiful were they, too, that words fail me in describing it."

A similar testimony was given by the visionary Marija on the feast of the Assumption, 1988. "On Apparition Hill late this evening," she said, "Our Lady came wearing a beautiful dress of gold. She was very pleased to see such a large crowd and blessed everyone. With her were three angels."

Again there were three angels accompanying the mother of God when she appeared to the visionary Ivan, on the night of 22 November 1988, in the chapel of Our Lady of the Angels – the convent chapel adjoining Mother Angelica's celebrated TV studio in Alabama.

Further testimonies
The Medjugorje locutionaries likewise testify to the presence and activity of angels in their own specific role – that of beholding Our Lady and other heavenly visitants interiorly and of hearing their messages, which they duly pass on for the benefit of others. To begin with, it was Jelena's guardian angel whose voice was heard during the week that preceded and prepared her for the coming of the Lord's mother in December 1982. Later, she would often see as many as six or seven angels surrounding Our Lady and hear them singing.

It has now become almost commonplace for Gospa of Medjugorje to come accompanied by angelic spirits – usually three but sometimes more. This especially applies to her late-night hillside appearances on Apparition Hill and Cross Mountain.

Mirjana reported a variation on the theme at her annual birthday apparition on 18 March 1991. "When Our Lady left me," she said, "the heavens opened and I saw three angels awaiting her there. Only once before – in August 1981 – had I seen angels waiting for her like this after she had been with us."

Clearly there could never be anything random or unplanned in the words and actions of her who is the Seat of Wisdom; rather, every single detail necessarily has its point and purpose. What, then, are we to read into the fact that God's mother brings the angels so regularly to our notice in Medjugorje?

The reality of angels

In the first place, Mary is reaffirming, for the benefit of a world which is becoming more and more entombed in materialism and plays down what is spiritual and supernatural, that angels really exist. More than that, they are closely and vitally relevant to human life and destiny. Our loving Father in heaven has given his angels charge over us to keep us in all our ways (cf. Ps 90:11).

Angelic beings form part of our God-given environment. "Millions of spiritual creatures walk the earth unseen, both when we sleep and when we wake." Milton's vision is the traditionally Christian one. Nobody was more aware of it than Pius XII. Shortly before his death in 1958, he exhorted pilgrims: "Try to awaken and sharpen your realisation of the invisible world about you, and foster a familiar acquaintance with the angels. You will spend, God grant it, an eternity of joy with them; so begin to know them now."

Similarly, the Medjugorje Madonna is lifting our eyes to the invisible angelic world which encompasses and environs our material one. She wants us to derive maximum benefit from what the angels stand to bring us – their ministrations, their companionship, their guidance, their protection, their inspiration. For this is their providential function *vis-à-vis* our human world. In St Paul's words: "All the angels are spirits apt for service, whom God sends out when the destined heirs of eternal salvation have need of them" (Heb 1:14).

Traditional truths

It is through faith, of course, that we perceive our angelic friends and communicate with them. Indeed, their reality is a credal truth, that is, one binding on our faith. We affirm it each time we profess belief in the Creator of "all that is seen and unseen". And the existence and ministrations of our unseen companions are firmly rooted, in the first place, both in the Old and the New Testament. The Church's long tradition and everyday liturgy amply confirm these truths. So does the Church's ordinary magisterium. Hence Vatican II was simply recalling an age-old practice when it encouraged us to "venerate the angelic spirits and invoke their intercession".

So our heavenly mother is here focusing our attention, in line with her Medjugorje pedagogy, on truths that are integral to Christian doctrine and devotion; however, they are sadly neglected nowadays and even denied by many in the name of theological progress.

The Queen of the Angels

The visionary Marija declares that, when the mother of God comes accompanied by angels, they are all rapt attention and loving devotion as they gaze at her unceasingly throughout the apparition. This throws an interesting sidelight on the fact that the angels are, in fact, Mary's loyal and affectionate subjects and show the deepest reverence towards her as to their queen.

For such she is. Pius XII dedicated an entire encyclical to her as "Queen of the Angels". And here he was merely giving expression to an ancient and universal tradition that honoured Our Lady under this title. Nor is it difficult to see its theological ground. As mother of the Creator, she also mothers all creation, the angelic included. And, as mother of the Redeemer, Christ the King, she shares in his royal dignity and thus exercises queenship and sovereignty over all heaven and earth.

As Vatican II phrased it, "the most holy mother of God was exalted by divine grace above all angels and mankind". Hence it arises, to quote Leo XIII, that the Virgin Mother exercises "her almost immeasurable power in the distribution of grace".

Woman clothed with the sun

The frequency with which Our Lady brings angels into the Medjugorje scenario reflects a further significant factor – one that is commonly met with in the pages of devotional literature both ancient and modern. It is that the angels, besides being Mary's devoted subjects, look up to her as their leader in the battle against Lucifer and his fellow fallen angels.

That is to say, Mary is the Woman of the Apocalypse; she is clothed with the sun; the moon is beneath her feet; and upon her head is a crown of twelve stars. Under her banner, Michael, the Archangel, rallies the angelic hosts in unrelenting battle against the Red Dragon – alias the renegade Lucifer, now Satan – and his demon hordes, the powers of darkness (cf. Rv 12:1-18). With good reason, then, the Medjugorje Madonna untiringly puts us on our guard against the formidable threat posed by the menace and might of these demonic forces. In message after message she urges us, above all, to pray – particularly the Rosary – that we may overcome those malign spiritual influences who are so active in our world these dark days (cf. Ep 6:10-12).

Our heavenly mother realises full well that we, her children, carry the treasures of heaven in that all-too-fragile earthenware which is ourselves (cf. 2 Co 4:7). So we must use every available weapon in God's armoury, including angel-power and angel-protection, to counter the strength and cunning of the evil spirits (cf. Ep 6:13-17).

It was from the Queen of the Angels herself that the visionary Vicka received the insight and wisdom to say: "We should ask God every single day to keep Satan at a distance from us. We should also make good use of the help God gives us through those angels he has assigned to protect us" (9 September 1990).

The Marian militia

The founder of the Marian Movement of Priests, Fr Stefano Gobbi, draws much of his inspiration from the frequent pilgrimages he makes to Medjugorje. One particular locution he is reported to have received from the mother of God (29 September 1981) fits this present context ideally; it applies as well to laity as to priests.

"In the struggle to which I am calling you," Our Lady's message runs, "you are being specially helped and defended by the angels of light. I am the Queen of the Angels. They have an important part to play in the struggle between myself, the Woman clothed with the Sun, and the Red Dragon. They are united with you in the terrible battle against the Dragon and his followers.

"These set dangerous and fearful snares for you, which you would not be able to escape without the special help of your guardian angels. That is why I call upon you to entrust yourselves more and more to the angels of the Lord. Have an affectionate intimacy with them, because they are closer to you than your friends and dear ones.

"Walk in the light of their invisible, but certain and precious, presence. They pray for you, walk by your side, sustain you in your weariness, console you in your sorrows, keep guard over your repose, take you by the hand and lead you gently along the road I have pointed out to you."

Faith in focus

Because it is faith alone which enables us to focus on the angel-world and hold dialogue with it, Our Lady of Medjugorje, who so champions the role of faith as such, will clearly be pleased, and we ourselves stand to benefit richly, the more light is thrown on her angelic subjects who, under her queenship, are devoted friends and powerful auxiliaries.

So let us briefly see something of the angels' nature, background and history, and of the close bond between their supernatural destiny and our own.

They are spiritual beings, endowed by the Creator with high

gifts of intellect and will. So, like ourselves, but at a finer pitch of being and doing, they are persons; that is, they are self-aware, self-reflective, self-deciding. Unlike our body-soul selves, however, they are pure spirits, having no admixture whatsoever of anything material in their composition or make-up.

For this reason we cannot picture the angels or imagine them visually or represent them in any concrete form. For, being wholly immaterial, they are invisible, intangible, right beyond the reach of our senses. That is why angels must necessarily assume some outward form when they appear, as is the case in both the Old and New Testament.

As for the wings which Christian art provided them with in medieval and earlier times, these were meant to symbolise the angels' swiftness of thought and movement. Indeed, St Thomas Aquinas and others affirm that angels become instantaneously present wherever they apply their mind and will.

It is also common teaching that God created a myriad of these mighty and beautiful angelic spirits. And a time-honoured tradition divides them into nine choirs or hierarchies; these are graded according to the respective natural gifts with which they were endowed by the Creator.

For or against God

Again it is common teaching that these splended celestial spirits were further endowed by the Creator with divine grace, its purpose being to enable them to comply with his will as made known to them, and so merit eternal life with him in the glory of heaven.

Whatever the actual scenario of their moral testing may have been, we know that a certain number of the angels failed it. That is, they abused their free will by rejecting God's terms. Their leader in this revolt against divine authority was Lucifer, one of the brightest stars in the angelic firmament. Pride ruled their wills. Perfectly aware though they were, thanks to their keen, intuitive, angelic intellects, of what the disastrous consequences would be, they revolted against God, thus turning their backs on the supernatural destiny he had offered them.

The Word Incarnate, who was as it were an eye-witness of that spiritual tragedy, later said: "I saw Lucifer fall like lightning from heaven" (Lk 10:18). And what Lucifer (now known as Satan) and his followers (now known as devils) fell into was a state, self-chosen and irremediable, of separation from God and of malevolence towards him and all his creation, especially his human images. We call that state and place hell.

The good angels, on the other hand, accepted God's holy will and duly merited the glory of paradise, which essentially consists in the Beatific Vision. Our Lord made reference to this in the text: "See to it that you do not treat one of these little ones with contempt: I tell you, they have angels of their own in heaven, that behold the face of my heavenly Father continually" (Mt 18:10).

Spirits apt for service

St Paul tells us that *all* the angels are ministering spirits in our regard (cf. Heb 1:14). In Our Lord's regard, too, angelic services were constantly provided in a variety of forms, all the way from the night of his birth to the day of his Ascension. In this context, Mother Angelica offers some helpful advice for gospel meditation. "It's good", she says, "to recall that your guardian angel actually witnessed Our Lord's whole life. So, if you have a problem meditating, ask him to inspire you about what happened."

As for angelic ministrations to Our Lord's followers down the centuries, they are legion. Already in the Acts of the Apostles we see what dramatic interventions were made by angels on behalf of Saints Peter, James and Paul.

In all their recorded apparitions in New Testament times, the angels seem to have assumed the standard appearance of young men in shining white garments (cf. Ac 1:10). Presumably, too, this is how the Archangel Gabriel presented himself to Our Lady at the Annunciation.

Privileged persons

St Frances of Rome, who lived in the fifteenth century, was privileged to see her guardian angel almost uninterruptedly over a span of several years. Here he chose to assume the form of a small child of great sweetness and beauty. His hands were crossed upon his breast; and he wore a long, shining robe over which was a tunic, its colour being white or rose-red or blue. Fascinatingly enough, this description tallies closely with that given by the Medjugorje visionaries of the angels they see there.

But these extraordinary cases are the exceptions that prove the rule: namely, the vast majority of us must be content with contacting the angels purely through faith. We never see, hear or touch them. For they belong essentially to the world of unseen realities, which is faith's home ground. And faith enables us to communicate with the angels spiritually; we do so, says St Thomas, "with our minds, imperfectly in this world, perfectly in the next".

Our angelic friends

A golden formula has come down to us from Pope St Leo the Great. "Make friends", he counsels, "with the angels." This inspired St Francis de Sales to write: "Make yourself familiar with the angels and behold them frequently in spirit. For, without being seen, they are present with you."

Besides being present with us, the angels can read our thoughts when directed towards them. What they can also read like a book is our memory, our imagination, and our external senses. And it is through these avenues, these portals, that the angels, in turn, can and do convey illuminations and guidance.

Very specially, of course, we should make friends with our God-given guardian angel, who, while beholding the face of God our Father unbrokenly in heaven, is constantly at our side as protector, guide, counsellor, companion, having received a divine commission or mandate to keep us in all our ways (cf. Mt 18:10; Ps 90:11).

Our guardian angels

This consoling truth has constantly been taught by the Church, which has even instituted a universal feast of the Guardian Angels, observed annually on 2 October. In its liturgy for that day, the

Church applies the thinking of St Thomas on the role of guardian angels; they represent, he says, "a particular application of divine providence" with regard to each one of us.

Nobody has understood and appreciated this comforting doctrine more keenly than Cardinal Newman. "I wish to have with you," he confided to his guardian angel, "conscious communion." And his childlike yet profound prayer runs: "My oldest friend, mine from the hour when first I drew my breath. My faithful friend, that will be mine, unfailing, until death."

What this wonderful mystery means, then, is that your loving Father in heaven has provided you, from birth till death, with a close friend and trusted escort and guide. He holds a divine mandate over you and your destiny. You are his charge, his ward, his protegé, his responsibility. He loves you intensely with a charity kindled in that sacred fire wherein his whole being is absorbed and glorified – the Beatific Vision. His powerful intellect knows you and your life-story down to the tiniest details. For he has been with you, watchful and unwearying, ever since you left your mother's womb. And he will remain with you, ever-vigilant and loving, till you breathe your last.

The Medjugorje message
The visionary Marija has special reason to recall an episode that occurred while she was away on holiday with three companions. During an apparition, Our Lady, having indicated that one of her companions was currently wanting to know more about the angels, expressed the wish that all four girls should compose a letter to their guardian angel, thanking him for all his services. When the mother of God appeared to Marija the following day, she was significantly accompanied by four angels!

In point of fact, there are five basic services which the angels perform on our behalf. And, by the happiest of coincidences, these services cover those very five areas mapped out by their Queen and ours in her Medjugorje message.

First, the angels help us to turn more fully towards God and to avoid sin at all costs. Our Lady, when instructing Jelena about saying the Lord's Prayer, proposed the angels as our models in making God's will the rule of our life (27 March 1985). St Frances of Rome noted that the least deliberate sin on her part would cause her guardian angel to disappear – pending her making an act of contrition.

The message's second item – faith – is similarly activated and energised through our contact with the angels. Their very existence, together with their providential role in our lives, registers with us in the first place directly through the agency of faith. And this supreme gift of God grows ever-stronger thanks to the healthy exercise it receives through our continuing contact and communion with the invisible angel-world.

Our angelic friends take a particular delight in seeing us draw closer to the Eucharist. For there we find him who is faith's author as well as its summit – Jesus, Joy of Angels: *panis angelicus* and also humankind's Bread of Life.

As for prayer and living in the presence of God, this third element in Our Lady's Medjugorje message finds in the angels its finest exponents and shining exemplars. Indeed, their foremost function in our regard is to protect and develop our prayer-life; that is, they variously teach, help, encourage, prompt, remind us to pray more and to pray better. Let us remember, too, that it is our guardian angel who presents our prayers to God (cf. Tb 12:12).

Penance and peace
The fourth plank in the Medjugorje platform, so to call it, is the practice of penance and self-denial, notably fasting. This being of such key importance in Christian spirituality, our angels foster it to the maximum degree, inspiring us to accept generously whatever crosses life may send our way, and to be brave and strong in "bearing in our bodies the mortifications of Jesus, so that the life of Jesus may be made manifest in us" (2 Co 4:10).

Two further texts come to mind here. These tell us, firstly, that angels came and ministered to Our Lord after his forty-day fast in the desert (Mt 4:11; Mk 1:13). Secondly, there must be immense joy among the angels of God over so many sinners doing penance – and also receiving regularly the sacrament which takes its name therefrom – in direct response to Our Lady of Medjugorje's call (cf. Lk 15:7).

Fifthly, there is peace, which, says St Augustine, is the very atmosphere of that paradisal city where the angels dwell. So, as they did at Bethlehem, they proclaim peace and spread it on earth. And they do so all the more zealously now that the Queen of Peace has made it her crowning gift in Medjugorje. Peace with the God of conscience, peace in our every human relationship, peace in our world – this is what the angels aim at and work for untiringly.

Harnessing angel-power

"Immaculate spouse of the Holy Spirit, by the power the Eternal Father has given you over angels and archangels, send all the angelic spirits, with St Michael at their head, to deliver us from evil and bring us healing."

Heaven responded swiftly and dramatically to this plea wrung from the heart of a hopeless young Italian drug-addict, Oberto Cattaneo, at the fourth station of the Cross on Cross Mountain one cold and rainswept morning in 1986. He suddenly felt himself overwhelmed with contrition for his past sinfulness and wept through sheer consolation. Moreover, he was soon to discover that he was now entirely freed from his slavery to drugs and alcohol. Angel-power had exerted itself instantly and in no uncertain way!

The poet is right when he says: "Tis your estranged faces that miss the many-splendoured thing." So many of us tend to overlook and neglect the ever-present angel-power that divine providence has placed at our disposal. If only we would implement St Bernard's counsel and be "assiduous in making contact, through our thoughts and prayers, with those who are ever at our side to guide and console us!"

St Bernard adds that, with regard to our guardian angel in particular, we should cultivate "reverence for his presence, love in response to his benevolence, and confidence in his power". This applies especially, of course, in moments of temptation, trial, danger, suffering, sorrow, depression, anxiety, stress, sadness and the like.

Some practical tips

Regarding devotion to your guardian angel, it is widely recommended that you give them a name of your own choosing; this can be masculine or feminine, since our wholly immaterial angelic friends belong to neither gender. This practice will not only express the intimately personal relationship between your angel and yourself but serve to deepen it.

A further recommendation concerns the Guardian Angel prayer: "Angel of God, my guardian dear, to whom his love commits me here, ever this day (night) be at my side, to light and guard, to rule and guide." As time and occasion allow, say this prayer slowly and piecemeal; that is, taking it phrase by phrase, as it were sipping and savouring the contents of each before passing on to the next.

We might note in passing that this so-called Ignatian method of prayer can usefully be applied to all well-known prayers, such as the Our Father, the Hail Mary, etc.

Several canonised saints and a number of recent popes are among those known to have followed the practice of greeting the guradian angels of others. An easy and effective way of doing so is simply to say, mentally, the Holy Name or the Glory Be in their honour. St Louis de Montfort even began every letter he wrote with the formula: "I greet your guardian angel." Our trust placed in their God-given power to help us is unfailingly rewarded by the angels, intent as they are on oiling the wheels of our everyday lives, with particular regard to human relations.

It was revealed to the Montreal mystic, Georgette Faniel, who has close links with Medjugorje, that there is a quite exceptional intercessory power in joint prayer offered on our behalf, if we ask them, by the entire heavenly court – that is, all the angels and saints: in a word, the Church Triumphant. And it is further recommended that we pray in unison with them, as indeed we do in the preface of every Mass when we say, "Holy, Holy, Holy...". Again, the Holy Name or the Glory Be commend themselves as easy and effective prayers for this purpose.

Closing prayer to Gospa

O Queen of the Angels, we thank you for stirring within us at Medjugorje a lively faith in the presence and power of your angelic subjects, and in the providential help and protection they supply on our long, hazardous pilgrimage through this world to the glorious City of God.

O Queen of the Heavenly Hosts, may your mighty archangels Michael, Gabriel and Raphael defend us in our warfare with the powers of darkness; and may they cast down to hell Satan and all wicked spirits who wander through the world for the ruin of souls.

O holy mother of God, help us through your prayers to remain ever-docile to the counsels and inspirations of those special celestial spirits – our very own guardian angels – whom your Son has appointed to keep us in all our ways.

Especially in the ways of repentance, faith, prayer, penance and peace – the substantials of your Medjugorje message, gracious Gospa – may the angels of God keep us all the days of our life.

7

The Menace of Satan

"What I tell you three times", says a Lewis Carroll character, "is true." Applying this dictum to Medjugorje, it follows that what Our Lady tells us there at least three *dozen* times must be all-too-true as well as highly important.

One of her early messages really says it all: "Satan exists and seeks to destroy" (14 February 1982). Hereby the mother of Christ affirms not only the reality of fallen angels but the deadly menace they pose for her Medjugorje plan as well as for humankind at large.

Clearly she is alerting us to something most relevant, sinister and threatening. St Paul referred to it as "the ever-active mystery of iniquity" (2 Th 2:7). And Pope Paul VI cautioned us to be on our guard against "the terrible, mysterious and frightening reality of evil purveyed throughout our world by living, spiritual beings who are perverted and cunning".

Over the entire human race, this sombre mystery casts a heavy shadow. One of the grimmest realities confronting the Church in every age, says Vatican II, is that "a monumental struggle against the powers of darkness pervades the whole history of man. The battle was joined from the very origins of the world and, as the Lord has attested, will endure until the last day. Caught up in this conflict, man is obliged to wrestle constantly if he is to cling to what is good. Nor can he achieve his own integrity without valiant efforts and the help of God's grace."

Talk of the devil
Before going any further, let us make an appropriate selection from what the Medjugorje Madonna has described as her "mosaic of messages". Thus we can savour something of their original inspiration and power.

- "A great struggle is about to unfold, a struggle between my Son and Satan. Human souls are at stake" (2 August 1981).

- "The devil is trying to conquer us. Do not allow him. Keep faith, fast and pray" (16 November 1981).

- "Do not allow Satan to gain control over your heart. For then you would become an image of him, not of me" (30 January 1986).

- "Satan is powerful. And he wants to destroy not only human life but nature and the very planet upon which you live" (25 January 1991).

- "I want you to listen to me and not let Satan seduce you. He is strong enough; but do not be afraid, because you are God's children and he watches over you. Pray, and let the Rosary be ever in your hands as a sign to Satan that you belong to me" (25 February 1988).

- "Ask everyone to pray the Rosary. With it in hand you will overcome all the troubles which Satan is trying to inflict on the Catholic Church. Let all priests pray the Rosary" (25 June 1985).

- "I invite you to place more blessed objects in your homes and to keep some blessed objects on your person. Thus Satan will attack you less because you will have armour against him" (18 July 1985).

- "You know that I promised you an oasis of peace. But you don't realise that beside an oasis stands the desert where Satan lurks, wanting to tempt each one of you. Dear children, only by prayer can you overcome every influence of Satan" (7 August 1986).

- "Always let love be your only instrument. Through love, turn everything into good which Satan seeks to destroy and possess" (31 July 1986).

- "Satan wants to work still more fiercely to take joy away from each of you. By prayer you can completely disarm him and ensure your happiness" (24 January 1985).

- "I call on each one of you to decide conscientiously for God and against Satan. I am your mother and therefore want to lead you all to complete holiness. I want each of you to be happy here on earth and to be with me in heaven. That, dear children, is the purpose of my coming here" (25 May 1987).

- "Dear children, I love this parish, and with my mantle I protect it from every work of Satan. Pray that he retreats from it and from every individual who comes here" (11 July 1985).

The two standards
This sub-title is borrowed from St Ignatius Loyola; it puts into a nutshell his view of the world and salvation history. He sees the human race as polarised between good and evil; that is, between Christ and Satan, the leaders of the two opposing camps or kingdoms perpetually pitted against each other as they fight for and against God respectively.

St Ignatius was well aware, of course, that Christ has vanquished Satan through his redemptive death, thus making available to us a super-abundance of supernatural benefits which are channelled through the Church. But St Ignatius was no less aware that Satan and his apostate angels work with might and main to block, so far as they can, the flow of those benefits to human beings; moreover, they seek to seduce them away from their allegiance to Christ and bring them under their own standard of evil and error.

It was from the gospel, of course, that St Ignatius drew his piercing insight into this scenario of dualistic, cosmic conflict between the powers of light and darkness. The same idea is expressed by St Paul; he urges us, as good Christian soldiers, to avail ourselves of every spiritual armament in the struggle against our unseen, unsleeping enemies. Similarly St Augustine: for him the whole panorama of human history is, at its profoundest level, the tale of two cities at war; one is loyal to God, the other to Satan.

It was only to be expected, then, that Our Lady of Medjugorje should frequently and urgently alert us to the formidable opposition we face from fallen angels. At the same time, and no less frequently and urgently, she bids us strengthen our defences through constant prayer and regular frequentation of the sacraments.

Truth for our times

The Queen of Prophets is once more using Medjugorje as a platform for proclaiming a revealed truth that has been seriously eroded in modern times. The devil exists – and exerts himself to damage human beings as much as he can in this world and, if possible, to bring about their eternal damnation in the next.

A good many Christians nowadays have been misled into dismissing Satan as pure myth. Or he is simply the personification of harmful tendencies in nature; not a personal being, therefore, but merely an impersonal force; not a living someone but a vague and abstract something.

Those theologians propagating such views run counter to long-established doctrines deeply rooted in Sacred Scripture, conciliar decrees, and the Church's everyday teaching. Add to this the massive testimony to the devil's reality and activity coming from that galaxy of great minds – the Church Fathers – in the early centuries. So let us be assured that demonology takes us into the daylight of revealed truth, not the shadow-world of mythology, folklore, superstition, or the like.

Light on a dark subject

For the added reason that the Medjugorje Madonna places such emphasis on these stark mysteries, she obviously wants us to grasp their meaning as fully as we can in the twin light of faith and reason. Furthermore, it is a principle of military strategy to learn as much as possible about your enemy, the better to do battle with him and emerge victorious. So let us see something of Satan's background and general track record.

Satan and his fellow-demons are angels, but fallen ones. That is, they belong to a higher order of creation than ours, having been endowed with a more powerful intellect and a stronger will. Moreover, being pure spirits, they are unbodied and wholly immaterial.

As is explained in the chapter on the angels, the Creator subjected them to a moral probation. With the help of divine grace they were to accept and obey the will of God as made known to them. Thereupon, as sequel and reward, they would merit eternal life in the paradisal world of the Beatific Vision.

We can only speculate as to the actual terms and circumstances of the angelic probation. One common theory is that the angels were given a preview, so to call it, of the mysteries of Bethlehem and Golgotha; that is to say, they beheld the Second Person of the Trinity as a helpless baby and as the Man of Sorrows. Would they, or would they not, continue to worship him in such abject abasement?

Anyhow, whatever its scenario, that primordial drama of angelic probation turned into unthinkable tragedy for some of them. Led by Lucifer, whose dazzling gifts reach the very peak of angelic perfections, and motivated by pride, self-love and disobedience, they rejected their Creator's will. They made what Dante called "the great refusal". Theirs was the first-ever sin. In Rahner's words, it was "the immense abyss of a sin occurring in a pure spirit".

Like a virus, the sin of the angels was destined to form the very contamination and evil root of all subsequent sins, human included. Essentially it was the sin of pride, aptly described by St Augustine as "love of self unto contempt of God".

Outcasts from God

Two things should be noted about the angels' sin. First, their

93

purely spiritual nature meant that their wills would make a once-for-all choice between good and evil, and that their choice would become fixed, definite, eternalised. Secondly, given the high-powered, intuitive intellect of the angels, they saw with blinding clarity the catastrophe that would ensue on their rebellion against God.

It is awesome to reflect that a good number of those resplendent angelic spirits, maliciously abusing their free will, and puffed up with obstinate pride, consciously opted for that condition of perpetual self-banishment from God which we call hell.

St John the Evangelist has graphically described that dramatic episode. He refers to Lucifer as "a great dragon, fiery-red, whose tail dragged down a third part of the stars in heaven". His account goes on: "Fierce war broke out in heaven, where Michael and his angels fought against the dragon. The dragon and his angels fought on their part, but could not win the day, or stand their ground in heaven any longer; the great dragon, serpent of the primal age, was flung down to earth; he whom we call the devil, or Satan, the whole world's seducer, flung down to earth, and his angels with him" (Rv 12:3,4, 7-9).

It was under the metaphor of lightning flashing across the sky that the Eternal Word was later to describe the fall of the angels (cf. Lk 10:18). And what Lucifer and his followers fell into was the exterior darkness of exile from God. There they now are, Lucifer and his lost legions, self-damned from here to eternity. The flames of their former charity have long since sunk into the cold ashes of hate and despair. In Milton's words, they say, as they contemplate Paradise Lost, "We outcasts from God are here to waste eternal days in woe and pain."

Lucifer is now known as "Satan" – a Hebrew word meaning adversary or enemy, since he is ever plotting against God and humankind. The general term for Satan and his satellite angels is "devil" – a derivation from the Greek word for calumniator, deceiver. Another common name for them is "demon"; this signifies that they are spiritual beings possessed of superhuman powers which they deploy maliciously and destructively.

The prince of this world

What ultimately accounts for the malign presence of Satan in our human world is his seduction of our first parents into committing original sin, the guilt and effects of which overshadow our lives from birth to death. As for original sin's damaging consequences, they are writ large across human history as well as our personal lives.

One of these consequences is that Satan now has a power-base here on earth. Thus the New Testament variously refers to him as "the prince of this world...the god of this world...the ruler of this world of darkness" (Jn 12:31; 2 Co 4:4; Ep 6:12). And St John declares roundly that "the whole world lies in the power of evil" (1 Jn 5:19).

Aware as she is of this situation, Mary Immaculate exhorts us in Medjugorje to become "reflections of Jesus, who will enlighten this unfaithful world that walks in darkness" (5 June 1986). For the powers of darkness are omnipresent and ever-active throughout the human story.

But these demonic powers are kept within strict limits by divine ordinance. That is to say, the fallen angels, though restlessly active in our world, are providentially kept on a leash – the leash of God's permissive will. We have a divine assurance that no temptation we experience will be beyond our grace-assisted power to resist (cf. 1 Co 10:13). At the same time, we have been repeatedly enjoined by our Medjugorje mother never to underestimate the devil's strength and resourcefulness (25 February 1988).

It is from Scripture that she takes her cue when she instructs us to arm and defend ourselves against the assaults of the enemy through faith, prayer and fasting (cf. 1 P 5:9; Mk 9:28). Like David facing up to the formidable Goliath, we are to keep in our hands that all-effective sling which is the Rosary (25 February 1988). The mother of the Church further advocates our maximum use of the Church's sacramentals, such as holy water, medals, scapulars, crucifixes and pictures, keeping them on our persons as well as in our homes (18 July 1985).

In mobilising the Church Militant for battle, Mary is equivalently recalling what St Paul told the Ephesians: "You must use all the weapons in God's armoury, if you would find strength to resist the cunning of the devil" (Ep 6:11).

Spiritual warfare

In an early apparition, Marija was informed by Our Lady: "A great struggle is about to unfold, a struggle between my Son and Satan" (2 August 1981).

What this amounts to saying is that Medjugorje has become a key zone, a vital sector, of the world-wide theatre of hostilities between the forces of good and evil. Under their respective leaders – "the woman clothed with the sun, the moon beneath her feet, with a crown of twelve stars upon her head", and "the great, fiery-red dragon" (Rv 12:1,2) – the angelic hosts and the demonic hordes are fighting it out.

St Paul was vividly aware of this non-stop clash between spiritual forces for and against God. Our terrestrial world is a battle-field on which good and evil are locked in mortal combat (cf. Ep 6:12). St Augustine envisaged this reality as a deadly warfare between two diametrically opposed cities – God's and Mammon's. As for St Ignatius, he had a panoramic vision of human history as a conflict, vast and unrelenting, in which Christ's kingdom is locked in deadly conflict with Satan's.

The Queen of Heaven is reported to have told Mirjana in 1982, following an extraordinary pseudo-apparition to her by Satan: "This century is under the power of the devil. But, when the secrets confided to you come to pass, his power will be destroyed. Even now he is beginning to lose his power and has become more aggressive. He is destroying marriages, creating divisions among priests, and is responsible for obsessions and murders."

Mirjana is on record that same year as having communicated this further message to a close friend: "The time has come when the devil is authorised to act with all his force and power. The present hour is Satan's."

That the spiritual warfare has intensified in our day was confirmed in a message received from the mother of God on 9

96

November 1984 by Fr Stefano Gobbi, founder of the Marian Movement of Priests. She predicted that the great struggle between herself and the Evil One would last throughout the twentieth century. Her enemy, she added, "felt certain that he would succeed in destroying the Church and in bringing all humanity to a universal rejection of God". But she went on to predict: "In the end, the pride of the Red Dragon will be broken by the humility, the littleness and the power of your heavenly mother, the Woman clothed with the Sun, who is now gathering all her little children into her army drawn up for battle."

Human souls at stake

Besides going on unabatedly around us, the warfare between the powers of darkness and of light is being waged *within* us – in that secluded theatre of hostilities each of us beholds all day and every day: our conscience. More than that, these opposing powers are fighting it out *over* us; that is, for the gaining, the winning, the possession of our souls; and this not merely during our mortal days but, immensely more important, throughout the endless eternity stretching out beyond death's horizon.

In Our Lady's words: "Human souls are at stake." Eternal issues – salvation or damnation – are in the balance. "Before a man are set life and death, and whatever he chooses will be given him" (Si 15:17). And the angels and demons, who have made their own irrevocable choice between the two eternities, are now intimately caught up, as friends and foes respectively, in the drama of our own personal destinies. Every passing day, and in an all-decisive way at the hour of his death, "the heart of man", in T. S. Eliot's line, "shivers and flutters between Heaven-gate and Hell-gate".

So the principal threat posed by the powers of darkness concerns our eternal salvation. Their malicious, murderous intentions in our regard are born of envy. It was from this source that, in the first place, sin came into the world at large, and the same holds for our private world of self. The root reason why the fallen angels are so consumed with envy is that we humans are destined to enjoy everlasting beatitude in that very paradise which they forfeited through their felony.

Eternal shipwreck

What further enrages Satan and his fellow-demons is that our created being is in the image of the Trinitarian Being whom they now detest so totally and blasphemously. In addition, we become, through grace, which is a sharing in that Being's very life, his living likeness and temples of his indwelling presence.

In the light of all this, we see more clearly why Our Lady of Medjugorje warns us about Satan so earnestly and so often. He and all the evil spirits are determined to drag us down with themselves into the city of damnation, the everlasting Gehenna, a glimpse of which was given to the visionaries by the Queen of Peace as a further salutary warning to us all. Our human souls are at stake. At all costs we must avoid becoming perpetual castaways with them of whom the poet wrote:

> Shipwrecked, they kindle on the coast
> False fires, that others may be lost.

Satan's strategy

The main false fires kindled on the coast of conscience by devils take the form of temptation, which is their stock-in-trade. The majority of theologians follow St Thomas in holding that devils cannot directly read our thoughts or violate our free will, since these are spiritual functions over which God alone has sovereignty. But they are able to tamper with our imagination, stirring phantasms liable to stimulate sinful thoughts and desires; also, they are capable of exciting and disturbing our bodily instincts, including the sexual and the aggressive.

In addition, the wicked spirits can stir and depress emotions as well as reach into the storehouse of memory so as to parade undesirable or disturbing images before our mind's eye. They know us inside-out, of course, including both our weaknesses and our strengths, and skilfully play on these for their own base purposes.

98

In her messages, the Virgin Mary specifies some of the methods resorted to by Satan in his bid to "block our path to holiness" (25 September 1987). He seeks to undermine our courage (14 January 1985), take away our joy (11 January 1985), bring about misunderstandings (25 January 1983), spread disorder (15 August 1983), cause hindrances (9 August 1984), generate frustration (12 July 1984), sow confusion (4 September 1986), and destroy peace (6 June 1986).

When reminding us that Satan is strong, the Madonna also has in mind his natural powers; these enable him to bring about some amazing effects in the material order of things. But he is limited as to the scope permitted him in any given case by divine providence. Indeed, Satan would bring about the destruction of planet earth, if he were allowed (25 January 1991).

Special activities
A demonstration of demonic power is seen in the methods used to intimidate St John Vianney over a period of thirty-five years. Devils produced such effects as terrifying apparitions, loud bangings, a range of animal noises, the burning of his bed, and a variety of other molestations. Much the same treatment was meted out to St John Bosco. And it is well known that the fallen angels sometimes beat Padre Pio mercilessly, leaving him lying in a pool of blood.

But the most serious incursion the powers of darkness can make against anyone is known as possession. This signifies that one or more demons actually indwell that person's body, laying siege to their external senses and also their internal powers of imagination and memory. Exorcism is the rite whereby possessed persons are delivered from the unclean spirit(s) lodged within them. Several exorcisms have been performed in Medjugorje.

Satan is anti-Medjugorje
"Satan wants to destroy everything you have received from me" (9 January 1989). This is one of the many occasions that the Queen of Peace has bidden us pray, above all, that Satan does not prevail over her in the Medjugorje parish, which is so vital and centrifugal

to her world-wide plan, and which she therefore protects under her mantle (11 July 1985).

Why the hostile hosts so loathe, fear and assault Medjugorje is that it is a spiritual stronghold, a citadel of Mary – the woman who crushes Satan's serpentine head and leads Michael and the angelic legions against the spirits of wickedness and error.

These malign forces realise only too well that the Woman clothed with the Sun has lit in this obscure village a mighty beacon of faith and holiness for the illumination and inspiration of the world-wide Church. No wonder, then, as she commonly warns in her messages, the powers of darkness strive so feverishly to infiltrate, thwart and finally destroy her Medjugorje plan (12 January 1984; 11 July 1985; 1 August 1985; 5 September 1985; 28 January 1987; 21 March 1988).

Clash of opposites

Just how starkly antithetical are the aims of Satan and the Woman clothed with the Sun can clearly be seen when we contrast his evil designs with her five-point Medjugorje message.

Mary bids us turn towards God and away from sin. Satan, on the other hand, would have us follow his own example by turning towards sin and away from God. Faith's value is extolled by Mary, whereas Satan seeks to erode it and distort its contents. We are called upon by Mary to fast and do penance; Satan, however, fosters unbridled self-indulgence and the gratification of every instinct and appetite. While Mary encourages prayer, Satan does all he can to discourage and deter us from its practice. Medjugorje has been established by Mary as "an oasis of peace" – God's peace in our consciences, our homes, our places of work, our world. But Satan works with feverish zeal to disturb peace, replacing it with guilt, anxiety, confusion, conflict, enmity, division, bitterness, unforgivingness, despair and – finally and everlastingly – the pain of loss in his own city of damnation.

Let us pray, above all, that Satan does not prevail over her in Medjugorje, which she therefore protects under her mantle (17 July 1985).

Closing prayer to Gospa

Shield us with your prayers, Medjugorje Madonna, against the assaults of our malicious enemies from hell. Make us strong in faith and persevering in prayer that we may overcome their every temptation and snare.

Mother of the Church, mobilise us into true and valiant Christian soldiers in our warfare with the powers of darkness. Keep us close to our ministering and loving friends and allies – Michael and all the angels – that we may benefit to the full from their protection, their comfort, their counsel, and their holy inspirations.

Win for us by your prayers, O Mother of Jesus, Terror of Demons, a deep devotion to him in his Eucharistic mysteries, that we may be strengthened in grace and stand firm against the powers of darkness.

O Queen of Prophets, continue to shield Medjugorje from every attempt by the evil one to damage it and distort its message. Keep us faithful to the Rosary, treasuring it as a mighty weapon in our spiritual warfare, and as a sign to Satan that we belong unreservedly to you, both in time and in eternity.

8

The Hour of our Death

An abiding impression pilgrims gain of Medjugorje is that, besides being most prayerful and peaceful, it is so vibrantly alive, joyous and youth-oriented. Only when you reflect more deeply on Medjugorje do you come to realise that, paradoxically, it is at the same time steeped in the mystery of death.

One of the main factors accounting for this is the high profile enjoyed by death in the everyday devotions and liturgy. In the first place, there is Medjugorje's favourite prayer – the Hail Mary – which is its very leitmotif and theme-song. Each time they recite it, countless pilgrim lips affirm the fact and the certainty of their death somewhere in the future, and ask the holy mother of God to grace that momentous hour with her presence and her prayers.

Similarly, in another oft-repeated Medjugorje prayer – the Hail Holy Queen – we look ahead to our rendezvous with death; our Christian hope points us exiles beyond its boundary to that homeland where our most gracious advocate will show us the blessed fruit of her womb, Jesus.

The death of Jesus
Deeply and intimately this is woven into the mystery of Medjugorje. For it is a stronghold of the Eucharist, besides being a Marian shrine. An endless stream of Masses makes Medjugorje into a well-spring of grace and holiness. This means that the death of the Lord is shown forth there, made present and applicable to our sinful selves, each of those many times that priestly lips pronounce the consecratory words over the bread and wine.

Then there is Medjugorje's Golgotha – the stark hilltop cross dominating, and shedding its benediction upon the busy pilgrim scene below. From its lofty eminence that cross bears silent witness to Good Friday, also inviting us to remain closely united with him whose death is our life.

Next there are those unforgettable stations of the cross. They are situated at intervals along the rugged, rocky route leading up to that cross-crowned summit. And they eloquently and poignantly portray the bitter events which culminated in the Saviour's death.

It was precisely on his deathbed, let us recall, that he made us the precious gift of his mother. In turn, she will unfailingly stand by our own deathbeds. Meanwhile, Mary's prayers support us on life's long journey, winning graces for each passing moment, each transitory now.

Nor could any grace be more practical and helpful than that which moves us to meditate upon the mystery of death. Many a saint, in fact, has made this a frequent practice. So let us now attempt such a meditation, asking Our Lady to illumine us with that special light she sheds in Medjugorje.

Death's certainty

This is the first thing to be affirmed about death, and we do so equivalently fifty times in every Rosary we say. At some unknown future hour we shall die; this is inevitable, inescapable. The only rock-bottom certainty we have in this world besides taxation, said Benjamin Franklin with wry humour, is the fact that death lies ahead.

Hopkins likened our breath to our *memento mori* – a reminder that some future breath will prove to be our last. Sooner or later night must fall – the night of death when our work of gaining merit will be brought to its close.

One of Medjugorje's most winning features is the attraction it has for young pilgrims, many still in their teens. You come across them there in their thousands, looking the picture of youthful vigour and radiating Medjugorje peace and happiness. Yet they, too, are destined to die one day. For, in Shakespeare's wistful words, "Golden lads and girls all must, as chimney-sweepers, come to dust."

A similar realism characterises our faith. It faces up to the fact that all human beings are mortal. Not a trace is to be found in it of the pagan attitude which treats death as taboo and unmentionable, sometimes even waxing bitter at the very thought of it: "Rage, rage against the dying of the light!"

Yes, Christianity looks death in the face. One of the facts of bodily life is that it will end one day. The machinery of our organisms will finally grind to a halt. When the body can no longer respond to the life-giving energies of its informing spirit, it becomes an inanimate corpse, dissolving into its component elements once its vital principle departs. It is biologically established that our organism starts to wear out after a certain age, to which process death comes as the climax. Christina Rossetti put it all into a nutshell when she said: "Mankind sets out a-dying from its birth."

Wisely, then, the Church gives us frequent reminders in her liturgy about death's inevitability, encouraging us at the same time to make all due preparation for it. "Dust thou art, and unto dust thou shalt return." The Ash Wednesday liturgy really says it all. So does Richard II in Shakespeare's play. One day, he says, we shall all have to exchange the large kingdom of life "for a little grave, an obscure grave".

Death's uncertainties
The visionary Mirjana, speaking in the light of what she knows about the ten secrets due to be fulfilled when the Medjugorje apparitions are over, stresses our need to be ready for death at any moment. This recalls that particular invocation in the Litany of the Saints which says: "Deliver us, Lord, from a sudden and unprovided death."

Incidentally, a medieval tag made the point that clerics commonly die unexpectedly: *Subitanea mors, clericorum sors.* One recalls here that an American pilgrim priest died suddenly in Medjugorje on 4 October 1989 – just before the commencement of the English-language concelebrated Mass.

What this all goes to show is that a strange paradox plays around death. That it will terminate each and every human life is an absolute certainty. But as for death's when, where and how, these are uncertainties shrouded in the mists of the future.

104

Our Lord himself pointed this out: we know neither the day nor the hour when we shall be required by God to give an account of our stewardship. As St Thomas More realised so well, we need to be ever on our guard against that ruthless thief – death – who will rob us of our precious bodily life:

> Death stealeth on full slily; unaware,
> He lieth at hand, and shall us all surprise,
> We wot not when, nor where, nor in what wise.

Constant vigilance

So our watchword should be viligance. Literally at any moment we could be summoned to leave this world. St Paul compares death to a wind that will blow away the frail, insecure tent of our earthly existence and waft us into the shelter of the home God has prepared; but that wind could come at any moment; therefore, we ought to be constantly at the ready (cf. 2 Co 5:2).

Nor is it only death's when and where that are unknown quantities; its how is equally so. "Death", in Webster's words, "hath ten thousand several doors for men to take their exits." Anyhow, whenever, wherever, and howsoever death comes into our life, we shall all unfailingly leave the stage of this world and appear before our Creator and Judge. "It is appointed unto man once to die, and after that the judgment" (Heb 9:27).

Because death will usher in the solemn moment of truth when we shall see ourselves as God sees us, we specially ask his mother to pray for us at that fateful hour. For it is the very crossroads of our destiny. Hence St Francis of Assisi's prayer: "Blessed are they, Lord, who are found walking by your holy will, for the second death will have no power to do them harm."

In her great school of holiness at Medjugorje, Our Lady's first and foremost lesson is faithfulness to God's holy will (10 July 1986). Besides being the recipe for a happy and holy life, it safeguards us against the dread reality of the "second death" – the death of a destiny in the City of Damnation.

Did Our Lady die?

The Church has never given a definite answer to this question. Rather, it leaves it open, as we see in the formula referring to Our Lady's assumption into heaven. This event took place, the dogmatic text declares, carefully maintaining its neutral stance in the debate, when Mary had "completed the course of her earthly life".

However, the mother of God is on record as telling the visionaries, in answer to their question on the subject: "I went to heaven before death" (12 October 1981). In other words, she was exempted from the penalty of death applying to humankind at large. For everyone born into this world contracts original sin, from which arises death as a penal consequence (cf. Rm 5:12). But Mary, through her Immaculate Conception, was not subject to this condition; nor, therefore, did she incur its penalty. Thus runs the argument advanced by the so-called Immortalists in favour of Mary's exemption from death.

The Mortalists, on the other hand, argue that Mary did die. They fully accept, of course, Mary's privileged status by reason of her having been preserved from all sin, both original and actual. And they further accept her consequent entitlement to exemption from the law of death.

But, even so, they go on to maintain, it was more congruent, that is, fitting and appropriate, for Our Lady to suffer death. For thereby she would identify personally with the death-experience undergone by her Son and due to be undergone by ourselves – the multitudinous, sinful children entrusted to her by the dying Saviour. On that occasion St John, the beloved disciple, stood proxy for us all. Like him, we now behold in Mary, as Our Lord bade us, our own beloved mother (cf. Jn 19: 26,27).

We good thieves

Yet another participant in that deathbed drama being enacted in the Good Friday darkness stood proxy for us. This was the Good Thief. We are represented by him inasmuch as we, too, are thieves – of the worst possible kind: we steal, through our sinfulness and neglect, from the due measure of homage, honour and service owing to God as our Creator and Redeemer.

A further reason why the Good Thief represents us is that he is suffering – a condition which is common to us all, since nobody is exempt from pain and sorrow. To put this another way: the cross comes into every human life, as it did literally in the Good Thief's case. A third reason for his representative role is that he is on his deathbed – a situation lying ahead for all of us on some unknown tomorrow.

A fourth reason is that the Mother of Christ attended at the repentant malefactor's deathbed, as she will at our own. In his moving meditation on this subject, Newman suggests that it was Mary's prayers that won for that dying sinner some wonderful graces. Not only did he repent of his misdeeds; he accepted his crucified condition as deserved divine punishment for them. "We receive no more than the due reward of our deeds" (Lk 23:41).

Finally, the Good Thief represents all those who obtain the grace of a happy death through being at peace with the God of conscience. Furthermore, he was uniquely privileged to hear, from the lips of the Sufferer alongside him, that most golden of promises: "This day you will be with me in paradise" (Lk 23:42).

The Krizevac sign

As we saw earlier, what serves to permeate Medjugorje with the mystery of death is the Eucharistic sacrifice offered there so numerously by pilgrim priests.

This is through the agency of a sacrament, of course – the Blessed Sacrament. But the Lord's death is further represented and brought vividly to mind through two sacramentals particularly cherished by the Lord's mother. Like all sacramentals, they are things that act upon us as occasions of grace by fostering faith and nourishing devotion (in this case to Christ's crucifixion and death), which they do through our senses and imagination.

The two sacramentals in question are the Krizevac cross and the crucifix as such. Our Lady specifically referred to them in a locution to Jelena: "The cross represents Christ; it is a sign pointing to him. The same applies to the crucifix you have in your home" (15 February 1984).

The cross standing on top of Mt Krizevac, like Golgotha gazing down on Medjugorje, is a thirty-foot-high cement structure perched on a wide plinth; it dates from 1933 – the Holy Year commemorating the nineteenth centenary of Christ's redeeming death. This project, Our Lady has told us, was providentially planned in the perspective of the apparitions due to start some fifty years later (30 August 1984).

The Medjugorje Madonna has also told us through the visionaries (whose testimony, though not infallible, we are nevertheless allowed by the Church to accept with human faith) that the Krizevac cross is for her a place of predilection; she herself prays frequently at its foot, requesting her Son to forgive our world its sins (3 November 1981). She goes on to exhort us to pray there in turn, because this cross, she explains, is central to what she is doing in Medjugorje (cf. 12 September 1985; 30 August 1984).

How central the Krizevac cross is to the Medjugorje scenario is borne out by the multitudes of pilgrims who, by day and by night, climb up there to unite themselves with the Christ of Good Friday and his sorrowing mother. As for the massive crowd that assembles on the summit for the annual Mass commemorating the Exaltation of the Cross, it benefits both by the sacrament and the sacramental of the Lord's life-giving death.

An additional indication of how central is the role of the mountain-top cross in the drama of Medjugorje is found in the frequency with which it features in the amazing secondary signs. Numerous eyewitnesses testify to seeing that cross do such things as disappear, or spin, or even be replaced by the luminous figure of the Virgin Mary.

Devotion to the crucifix

The crucifix is the second sacramental much favoured and recommended by our heavenly mother as a means of bringing the Lord's death before our minds and hearts. A good many times she pleads with us to practise this devotion.

To quote some examples: "Pray as much as you can before a crucifix. Contemplate the wounds of Jesus" (20 March 1989)..."Pray especially before the crucifix from which come great graces" (12 September 1985)..."You must renew praying before a crucifix. Dear children, I give you special graces from there, and Jesus confers special gifts" (20 February 1986).

Our Lady is further on record as proposing that we say a Rosary in front of a crucifix and, too, make it the occasion of giving thanks to God for all his benefits (13 April 1990). In one instance, she invited Ivan's prayer-group to spend as much as two hours daily in prayer before a crucifix (28 March 1988).

In a locution to Jelena the mother of God said: "It is beautiful that you venerate the cross each Friday" (25 May 1983). Hereby she referred to a public devotion in the church that she warmly commends, namely, the holy hour known as Adoration of the Cross; it follows the Eucharistic liturgy on Friday evenings.

It is said that the first Christian emperor, Constantine, having been given a vision of a cross in the sky before his decisive military victory, subsequently placed a cross of gold adorned with precious stones in the chief hall of his palace. Similarly, Our Lady of Medjugorje is exalting the cross – emblem of her Son's redeeming death and victory over sin – to a position of exceptional prominence and honour in the halls of holiness and apostolate.

The grandeur of death

The Medjugorje Madonna is reported to have told the visionary Vicka, in response to a question posed by Fr Tomislav Vlasic, that at the moment of death we are fully conscious of the soul's separation from the body (24 July 1982).

This certainly chimes in with death's dignity as journey's end to the long marathon of life. Death is that moment of truth when our lifetime pilgrimage ends and we stand poised to enter the shrine, the sanctuary that we long for and aspire after here below. Scripture supplies a fitting text for this great moment: "The scene of your approach now is Mount Sion, is the heavenly Jerusalem, city of the living God; here are gathered thousands upon thousands of angels; here are the spirits of just men, now made perfect; here is Jesus, the spokesman of the new covenant" (Heb 12:22-24).

Deathbed rehearsal

Through being faithful to God's grace, we shall be able to say on our deathbeds, as did our dying Saviour, "It is consummated." Our lifework for God will be over. And our hoped-for epitaph will be, in Shakespeare's words, "Thou thy wordly task hast done; home art gone, and taken thy wages".

So death is the goal we are making for throughout life. It is the North Star upon which the compass of Christian faith is set. "For me," said St Paul, "life means Christ; death is a prize to be won" (Ph 1:21).

This Christian conviction was expressed in a somewhat more down-to-earth way by the popular Dominican preacher, Fr Vincent McNabb. He said to the reporters interviewing him on his deathbed: "What the blazes are you all looking so sad for? This is the moment I've been living for and praying for all my life!"

Death is the very crossroads of destiny. Milton described it as "the key that opens the golden palace of eternity". Hence it is the most solemn and decisive moment of our life. Hence, too, we so assiduously invoke the prayers of our heavenly mother that the hour of our death will be our lifetime's finest hour. We must glorify God in our death, St Ignatius exhorts us, as much as we do in our lives.

Our personal Good Friday

So Medjugorje introduces us profoundly into the mystery of death – Our Lord's and our own. Chesterton wrote some memorable words about Christ's lifework and goal in this world: "The gold that he was seeking was death. The primary thing that he was going to do was die. We are meant to feel that his life was in that sense a sort of love-affair with death, a romance of the pursuit of the ultimate sacrifice."

That ultimate sacrifice not only broke the menace of the "second death" – separation for ever from God in the City of Damna-

110

tion. It also took the sting out of the "first death", namely, the separation of soul from body. The magic wand of the Saviour's redeeming grace has been waved over death's grim form, transfiguring it from tragedy into triumph, transforming its terror and desolation into a sacrament of peace aglow with the prospect of heaven ahead.

So death is no longer the hag that rides the dreams of pagans ancient and modern; rather, like St Francis, we can greet it as "our little sister". That most apostolic soul, Pauline Jaricot, said she feared debt more than she did death. The ground for this confidence is indicated in St Therese of Lisieux's words: "It is not death that will come to fetch me, but the good Lord himself."

Therefore, when our personal Good Friday arrives, and the darkness of death starts to pervade our being, and we are about to take that momentous step into the mysteries beyond, we must place absolute trust in our merciful Lord. And we must make our own his perfect deathbed prayer: "Father, into your hands I commend my spirit" (Lk 23:46).

Moreover, the Lord's mother and ours will preside lovingly over our deathbeds, praying for us in response to our every Hail Mary. The psalmist's words will then be fulfilled: "Precious in the sight of the Lord is the death of his holy ones" (Ps 116:15). And Browning's verse will find full verification:

> You never know what life means till you die.
> 'Tis death that makes life live.

Death is our birthday

As the inscriptions in the Roman catacombs bear out, the early Christians commonly described the day we die as *dies natalis* – our birthday into eternal life. Death will usher us, the new-born, into the mysteries, the splendours, the inconceivable wonders of the world to come. Nobody was more excited about this than St Catherine of Genoa. "When I see someone die," she wrote, "I think within myself, 'O what great and wonderful things his soul is going to see!' "

111

The very thought of those great and wonderful things used to send St Ignatius into ecstasy. But, being an eminently practical man, and realising that this experience, privileged though it was, created backlogs in his very heavy workload, he decided to forego that luxury in favour of the more prosaic demands of daily routine!

The Church's liturgy for what Lacordaire called "the most beautiful day of our lives" gives us an insight into the initial stage of our post-death journey. "Come to meet him, O angels of the Lord. Welcome his soul; present him to God the most high."

This inspired Newman's sublime vision of the guidance given to the soul of Gerontius, newly-arrived in the next world, by that most loving and gentle of escorts – his guardian angel.

For many of us, no doubt, the first destination to which our angelic guide will need to conduct us is purgatory – that mysterious realm midway between earth and heaven. It is a world of reparation for sin and of purification from sin's ill-effects on the spirit. At the same time, it is a world of prayer and, above all, preparation for entry into paradise. The Holy Souls' ardent aspirations echo what the Curé d'Ars would often exclaim in sheer wonderment: "O blessed Trinity, we shall actually *see* you!"

The resurrection of the body

"I believe in the resurrection of the body and life everlasting." In these two concluding articles of the Creed our faith attains its very climax and crown. And in Medjugorje these particular credal articles enjoy a high profile – for two reasons.

First, the Madonna of Medjugorje has already experienced the resurrection of her body and is enjoying life everlasting. She is radiantly beautiful and youthful, the visionaries tell us, having been assumed body and soul by her Risen Son into the glory of paradise; this was both privilege and reward for her unique dignity as sinless mother of the Word Incarnate.

The second reason why our bodily resurrection and enjoyment of eternal life are so highly profiled in Medjugorje is that the Eucharist plays such a dynamic role there. And the Eucharist, as

Our Lord has declared, is directly linked with our own resurrection.

To begin with, he is present with his risen humanity, which is the pattern and pledge of our own. In the second place, he is present as our Eucharistic food for the long Emmaus road of life, nourishing our faith, warming our charity, and reinforcing our "hope of achieving resurrection from the dead" (Ph 3:10). Indeed, he has given us an assurance that, if we eat his flesh and drink his blood, he will raise us up on the last day (cf. Jn 56:55).

Golden lads and girls

So Medjugorje provides a powerful tonic for our faith in the God of the Resurrection. By reason alone and the universal conviction of humankind we know that the human spirit is of its very nature imperishable, immortal. But the wonderful Easter tidings tell us that not only our spirits will be glorified everlastingly in God; our bodies, too, will share in that same shining destiny.

"The body, drawn from the earth" said Our Lady in an early message, "decomposes after death. It never comes back to life again. Man receives a transfigured body" (24 July 1982).

St Paul said exactly the same thing. Our Risen Lord, he wrote, "will form this humbled body of ours anew, moulding it into the image of his glorified body" (Ph 3:21).

Yes, our bodies will be humbled beyond recognition in the great democracy of death. In Shakespeare's words, "mean and mighty rotting together have one dust". But for those who, like Martha, have faith in him who is the Resurrection and the Life, our human dust will be transmuted into stardust. When the angels of the Parousia and Judgment Day sound the grand reveille, awaking countless legions of sleeping Lazaruses into new life, we shall become immortal diamonds. Once born into the brave new world to come as "children of the resurrection" (Lk 20:36), we shall be golden lads and girls, destined never again to come to dust.

Closing prayer to Gospa

Loving Mary of Medjugorje, mother of God and mother of mine, pray for us sinners now and at the hour of our death. Intercede, O merciful Gospa, for those who are destined to die this day, this night. Fill us, loving mother, with zeal for living your message and spreading it to others.

O gracious Queen of Peace, guide us, through life and through death, to the shining destiny awaiting us in the world of eternal happiness, the world of the resurrection from the dead.

9

A Window on Purgatory

As is well known, Our Lady has shown the Medjugorje visionaries (as she did their Fatima counterparts) something not only of heaven and hell but of purgatory as well. This was to bring home to them – and, through them, to us – the reality of that mysterious, wistful world of penal suffering and purification. Besides promoting our faith in purgatory, God's mother is stirring our compassion towards the holy souls and moving us to help them through prayers and sacrifices.

Messages about purgatory
Let us first see what Our Lady has said on the subject:

● "Dear children, there are many souls in purgatory. Among them are persons who have been consecrated to God – some priests, some religious. Pray for their intentions at least seven Our Fathers, Hail Marys and Glory Bes, plus the Creed. I recommend this to you. There are a large number of souls who have been in purgatory for a long time because no one prays for them" (21 July 1982).

● "Dear children, today I invite you to pray daily for the souls in purgatory. Prayer and grace are needed by each soul for it to reach God and his love. By doing this, dear children, you win for yourselves new intercessors who will help you to realise that all earthly things are unimportant, and that we should strive only to reach heaven. Therefore pray without ceasing so as to benefit both yourselves and those others to whom your prayers will bring joy" (6 November 1986).

● "Dear children, the souls in purgatory await your prayers and sacrifices" (1 November 1983).

The reality of purgatory

Here our faith and devotion are being focused by our Medjugorje mother on a much-neglected dogmatic truth – one that is abundantly backed up by Scripture and traditional teaching, including some conciliar definitions. Further backing is supplied by the Church's everyday belief and practice, as is evidenced in her public liturgy and the private devotions of the faithful.

Purgatory's reality has been reaffirmed in our own day by Vatican II. It declared: "We accept with great devotion the venerable faith of our ancestors regarding this vital fellowship with our brethren who are in heavenly glory or who, having died, are still being purified."

So powerful is the light of revelation that it also illumines the landscape across death's horizon, showing us there, in addition to heaven and hell, a zone, a realm called purgatory. There, as in a prison or penal settlement, disembodied human spirits in their multitudes undergo cleansing punishment in expiation of the debt each owes divine justice because of their sins (the guilt of which has already been forgiven). Through this process of purgatorial punishment and purification, the holy souls are progressively prepared for entry into paradise.

Meanwhile, we members of the Church Militant – that is, the Church in this world of time and probation – can offer prayers and suffrages for the relief (and, in certain circumstances, even the release) of our brothers and sisters in the Church Suffering, as purgatory is called. The official teaching in this regard was formulated by the Council of Florence: "The souls detained in purgatory are helped by the prayers of the faithful and, above all, by the holy sacrifice of the Mass."

Approaches to purgatory

The Council of Trent offers some very sound advice with regard to any discussions about purgatory, particularly in popular expositions. It tells us to avoid subtle and difficult aspects that are not going to prove helpful. It likewise frowns on whatever savours of idle curiosity and superstition, besides, of course, anything scandalous or repulsive.

Readers can be assured that nothing of this kind is met in what Medjugorje offers on the subject of purgatory. To begin with, it is perfectly in accord with what the Church's magisterium tells us. Moreover, the light cast on purgatory by Medjugorje's private revelations blends perfectly with what some of the classic mystics have said about that mysterious world beyond death's horizon.

As for theological speculation about purgatory, it goes back to the patristic era and has been enriched by some of the most distinguished names in the history of theology. Such speculation is entirely valid, of course, provided it remains within the framework set by the Church's magisterium. And, as we shall shortly be seeing, theological speculation draws much additional illumination from what private revelations provide. Thus, thanks to these various sources, we receive what Rahner terms "considerations that prove helpful towards an understanding of purgatory".

Visionaries testify

All six have been shown something of purgatory, Vicka and Jakov notably in November 1981. They explain that Our Lady did not take them inside purgatory but simply let them see it from without. There is a close similarity between the various impressions recorded by the six seers. They are to be found in a number of interviews, notably Jan Connell's classic *Queen of the Cosmos* and Fr Janko Bubalo's work, *A Thousand Encounters with the Virgin Mary*.

Certainly it is Vicka's description of purgatory that is the fullest and most vivid. It is a vast, austere, abyss-like space between heaven and hell, ash-grey in colour, melancholy, swathed in fog and mist, formidable and terrible to behold. And it is full of human spirits. "We could not see them," Vicka reports, "but we were aware that they were weeping, moaning and trembling amid terrible sufferings." Vicka further reports Our Lady's exhortatory words: "These poor souls need your prayers, especially those with nobody to pray for them." What we also learn from Vicka is that "the holy souls can see us on earth only when we pray for them, by name".

Marija's account of purgatory tallies closely with that of Vicka. It is an immense desolation, grey, gloomy, grim, obscured by fog and mist. "You cannot see the holy souls there," Marija comments. "It is as if they are immersed in deep clouds." She goes on to say: "They can pray for us but not for themselves. They are desperately in need of our prayers...I heard a lot of voices begging for our prayers. They are looking for our prayers to help them enter heaven sooner. Our Lady told us to pray very often for them, and to make sacrifices and attend Mass for their sake."

Ivan is on record as saying: "Souls in purgatory suffer. If nobody prays for them, they suffer for a longer time." And he adds the wistful comment: "Our Lady has said that the holy souls are extremely lonely."

What we learn from Mirjana is, as we would expect, practical and to do with prayer. "The Blessed Mother", she says, "has asked us to pray for the souls in purgatory. They are helpless to pray for themselves. Through prayer we on earth can do much to help them."

Ivanka and Jakov were characteristically laconic in their observations about purgatory. Ivanka simply said that it is "only darkness" and we must pray for the holy souls. As for Jakov, he supplied us with a little gem of wisdom. Asked whether we, like himself, should pray for the holy souls, he replied: "Yes, as an act of love."

Purgatory and ourselves

"There are some who depart this life," wrote St Augustine, "not so bad as to be deemed unworthy of mercy; nor so good as to be entitled to immediate happiness in heaven."

Many of us would instinctively feel that we belong to this middle category. That is, we would expect eternal life to be deferred in our case until we had undergone a prior period of purification and penance. Through God's grace we shall die in his peace; but in all likelihood we shall still be in his debt as regards the reparation due on the sins he so mercifully forgave us during our lifetime. Like Gerontius, we shall "join the souls in prison for the unpaid debt on sins committed here".

So purgatory, far from being abstract and academic, is a most practical and relevant subject on Our Lady's Medjugorje list of lessons. *Mea res agitur.* It concerns me personally, vitally. For it has much to do with reparation, namely, making amends to the God of justice on account of my violations of his commandments.

Reparation is the equivalent of expiation, satisfaction, penance. And a measure of it is demanded by each and every sin. So the duty of doing penance is incumbent upon all our sinful selves. This can either take the form of mortifications and self-denials we voluntarily impose upon ourselves, or it can be the offering of whatever trials, tribulations and sufferings life sends our way.

We see, then, why penance features so integrally in the Medjugorje message. We also see its value as being an anticipation here on earth of purgatory. And because purgatorial pain is far more intense than anything to be experienced here below, we are counselled by St Robert Bellarmine and others to take maximum advantage of this favourable ratio. That is to say, we should learn to use this present world as an outpost of purgatory. The beautiful old medieval prayer, the Jesus Psalter, teaches us the same lesson. "Jesus, Jesus, Jesus," runs one of its invocations, "send us here our purgatory."

Purgatory and our dear ones
Our Lady expressly told Mirjana to pray in a special way for her deceased relatives and friends, and to bring them joy and solace by attending Mass on their behalf (28 January 1987). Vicka said in an interview that similar instructions had been given her.

We see here a further reason why purgatory touches our own lives so intimately. Some much-missed dear ones, as well as old friends and colleagues, are very possibly among that immense multitude detained by divine justice in those penitential and purifying flames. Our sweet and tender mothers and kind, loving fathers; our brothers and sisters and other members of the family circle; all those unforgettable people whose lives became interlinked with our own – a whole cavalcade of persons here comes to mind. So do Tennyson's words:

> Oh for the touch of a vanish'd hand,
> And the sound of a voice that is still!

We see their faces smiling at us through the mists of memory, and we mourn them deeply. But, thank God, far from being cut off entirely, we can build a bridge of faith, dialogue, love and solidarity to them in their helpless condition as holy souls. Above all, the sacrifice of the Mass sends a refreshing stream of solace and relief into the bitter pains they are enduring.

Furthermore, as we shall presently see, we can gain indulgences for the holy souls, including the golden gift of a plenary indulgence; this confers the equivalent of a total amnesty upon some privileged detainee in that divine penitentiary, bringing about their instant release and admission to the glory of heaven (see Appendix, p. 157, for conditions required).

Purgatory's pain of loss

As the visionaries have seen for themselves, there is much pain as well as pathos in that twilight world where untold numbers of departed souls lament their past sins and undergo an expiatory cleansing on their account.

Technically there are two kinds of pain experienced in purgatory, so giving rise to its name: the Church Suffering. The first is the pain of loss, so called because, though only temporary, it is felt as a deprivation of the Beatific Vision. Purgatory's inmates, now more conscious than ever before of God's infinite perfections and desirability, suffer an ardent longing for him.

Moreover, their longing is rendered all the more intense by the complete freedom they now enjoy from all temporal distractions and cares, as well as by their being no longer subject to the inertia and downward drag of the body and its senses. Add to this their keener awareness of God's holiness and sin's offensiveness.

The visionary Marija was favoured with an insight into this pain of loss. "The holy souls' biggest suffering", she said in the Jan Connell interview, "is that they see there is a God but did not accept him here on earth. Now they long so much to come closer to him. Now they suffer so intensely because they recognise how much they have hurt God, how many times they have disregarded him, and how many opportunities they wasted."

Purgatory's pain of sense
Because it is a positive pain of a material kind inflicted nonetheless on immaterial human spirits, this second kind of purgatory-pain is termed the pain of sense. It is commonly held to be physical fire, albeit wholly different from anything known to us on earth; also it is able to constrain and inflict pain upon separated spirits.

So severe is the pain of purgatory that its minutest particle, St Thomas teaches, is far worse than the heaviest imaginable suffering on earth. Indeed, he goes on to say that it is even severer than anything Our Lord suffered during his bitter passion.

These and similar statements by theologians are corroborated by the testimony of mystics. For example, the seventeenth-century Carmelite, St Mary Magdalen of Pazzi, said that words failed her in describing the torments of purgatory. In comparison with them, she said, "the dungeons of the martyrs are gardens of delight".

Catholic traditional teaching is that in purgatory there are degrees of suffering, measured as well in terms of duration as of intensity. And these degrees correspond to the amount of penance and purification required of each soul by the God of justice and holiness.

This proportional dispensation of divine sanctions is confirmed by Mirjana in the almost Dantesque impression she gained of purgatory. "There are several levels", she said in the Jan Connell interview. "The lowest is the closest to hell, where the suffering is the most intense. The highest level is the one closest to heaven, and there the suffering is the least. What level you are on depends on the state of purity of your soul. The lower the people are in purgatory, and the less they are able to pray, the more they suffer. The higher a person is in purgatory and the easier it is for him to pray, the more he enjoys praying and the less he has to suffer."

God's holiness and justice

Among the important lessons to be drawn from purgatory's rigorous school of suffering is that God is all-holy and all-just. His infinite holiness is reflected in the sheer severity of purgatorial sanctions. For sin, even the most venial, is essentially an offence against the divine holiness; and purgatory's pains are essentially penal with regard to sins that have been committed.

Purgatorial punishment is equally a pointer to God's justice. for he strictly demands due reparation in respect of each sin, ready though he is to forgive the guilt attaching to it.

Come to think of it, this principle – punishment to fit the crime – is inherent in every system of law, since without it they would become mere "paper tigers" that offenders could transgress with impunity. How much more properly, then, must it not apply to the divine law, which is the source whence all moral and legal systems take their origin.

Indeed, we recognise the principle's living application in the very existence of purgatory. For it is that prison where offenders against God's law must pay him, the just Judge, the very last farthing of reparation – in union with the superabundant reparation for sin made by our Redeemer – before they can be admitted to the Beatific Vision (cf. Mt 5:26).

Purgatory purifies

Purgatory's penal aspect tells us what an offence against God sin must be for it to incur from him such dire sanctions. Purgatory's cleansing role, on the other hand, brings home to us what soiling and damaging effects sin must have on the human spirit for such a thorough purification to be required.

Actually, purgatory's underlying purpose is indicated in its very name, which derives from the Roman military term for a wash-house: *purgatorium*. "The holy souls", as the Council of Lyons summed it up, "are punished with the punishments of purification."

"Nothing defiled shall enter heaven" (Ws 7:25). Thus purgatory can be likened to a divine crucible in which the dross of sin's effects is consumed, leaving the pure gold of holiness. Or we may compare the human soul to an immortal diamond that has been flawed by sin and needs polishing before being presentable before God.

"The communication of the dead", it has been said, "is tongued with fire beyond the language of the living." What, then, are the holy souls telling us in the silent language of faith and love? Their message is simple and stark: "Avoid sin at all costs. For it not only displeases God but wounds and soils you in your deepest self. It demands dreadful punishment. It necessitates a drastic process of healing and cleansing. It delays your admission into the glory of paradise."

Good thieves and chimney-sweeps

To quote what was said in the chapter on death, the Good Thief who died alongside Our Lord stood proxy for us, "because we, too, are thieves – of the worst possible kind; we steal, through our sinfulness and neglect, from the due measure of homage, honour and service owing to God as our Creator and Redeemer".

Similarly, the souls in purgatory are so many Good Thieves who have made their peace with God. Moreover, they are hanging on a cross of pain and purification, suspended between this world and heaven. And what they say, adapting their prototype's words, is: "We suffer these purgatorial things deservedly on account of our sins. Also we suffer them necessarily in order that sin's harmful effects within us may be undone."

In that bright light cast by purgatory's purifying fires, the holy souls see all too clearly that, like so many chimney-sweeps, they need a thorough washing and grooming before being admissible to the royal court of paradise. They make the psalmist's words their very theme-song as they prepare for their day of deliverance: "Wash me clean, cleaner yet, from my guilt; purge me of my sin,

123

the guilt which I freely acknowledge, the sin which is never lost to my sight" (Ps 50:4,5).

Purgatory's keen flames reach down into the hidden recesses of our inmost selves, purging us of sin's after-effects – its multiple vestiges, defilements, blemishes, stains, scabs and scars. This sorry state of affairs is the result of a lifetime's sinfulness – our deep-rooted attachment to forbidden things, our ingrained bad habits, our stubborn pride and prejudices, our self-indulgences, our sinful passions, our neglect of grace, our flirtations with evil, our laxity, our lukewarmness, our slowness and sluggishness in God's service, our self-centredness, our arrogance, our failures in charity, our dishonesty and untruthfulness, our rebellions against God's will, our unfaithfulness to duty, our mediocrity, our poor performance as disciples and apostles.

Purgatory's peace and joy

As we have seen, purgatory is a world of pain – pain that punishes, purifies, and prepares sin-soiled souls for their eternal destiny. The wounds of sin are cauterised with surgical precision and healed in the fires of divine holiness and justice; thereby human spirits are rendered fit and ready to enter into and enjoy the glory of God.

But a strange paradox prevails in purgatory. Though healing pain is writ large across the landscape, its inmates are at the same time bathed in deep peace and joy. Thus St Catherine of Genoa, who had a mystical experience of purgatory, likened it to "a sweet prison, a holy sepulchre". The holy souls, she explains, are filled with joy as they become increasingly united with the divine will. She even claims that "their joy cannot be compared with anything except the greater joy of paradise itself".

St Francis de Sales says exactly the same thing. "From the thought of purgatory," he writes, "we may draw more consolation than apprehension. We must not think of the sufferings without also considering the peace and happiness enjoyed by the holy souls. Their torments, it is true, are so great that the most acute sufferings of this life bear no comparison with them; however, the interior satisfaction enjoyed there is such that no earthly prosperity or contentment can equal it."

What explains this, the saint continues, is that the holy souls are unbrokenly in union with God and conformed to his will. And, because God's holiness demands it, they purify themselves willingly and lovingly. Further, they are assured of their salvation through being confirmed in grace and therefore no longer in danger of committing sin. Meanwhile, too, they enjoy the consoling company of their guardian angels.

"The bitterest anguish experienced by the holy souls," the saintly bishop concludes, "is soothed by a certain profound peace. Thus purgatory is a species of hell as regards the suffering; but, as regards the delight infused into their hearts by charity, it is a paradise."

Purgatory's paradox

So we are confronted here with an amazing paradox. On the one hand, as the Mejugorje visionaries, among others, testify, purgatory is a dour, dire penitentiary wrapped in mists and melancholy. Yet, on the other hand, the most reliable authorities assure us that, its penitential suffering notwithstanding, purgatory is suffused with peace, sweetness and joy.

This co-existence of such opposites in the purgatory experience becomes less of a mystery when we reflect, as Suarez bids us, that the Crucified Saviour never for one moment lost his divine peace. And he imparts it in abundant measure, along with his joy, to the members of his mystical body undergoing spiritual crucifixion in purgatory.

Similarly, to his martyrs here on earth the Crucified Lord gives abundant peace and joy; thus we commonly read that, in the midst of physical torments, they experienced choice consolations from heaven. Likewise to many a suffering member of his Church the Man of Sorrows extends abundant compensatory graces. A good many of us have been privileged to come across invalids and sufferers who, burdened though they are with crosses of the heaviest kind, nevertheless radiate peace, serenity, joy and cheerfulness.

Helping the holy souls

In focusing our faith and our charity on the souls in purgatory, the Medjugorje Virgin is invoking the beautiful mystery known as the Communion of Saints. This stands for the bond, the unity, between all Christ's members in heaven and purgatory and on earth. Accordingly, we can forge links of love and prayer with our brothers and sisters both in this world and the next.

As was noted earlier, the Medjugorje visionaries heard the holy souls wistfully imploring our prayers for their relief. We also noted that Our Lady singles out Mass (even if we only attend it) as being the most effective suffrage we can offer.

Here God's mother is echoing a distinguished chorus of voices ever since the Apostolic Age. St Cyril of Jerusalem, for example, declares that the holy souls "receive very great benefits while this holy and tremendous Victim lies on the altar". And St John Chrysostom states quite categorically: "The Eucharistic sacrifice is the best way of bringing relief to the dead." Nor did anybody appreciate this more than St Monica. For she specially asked her son – St Augustine – to remember her while he was saying Mass.

Our common wealth

The Mass's whole meaning and efficacy lies in the fact that it is the sacrifice offered by him who is head of the mystical body. Now this body is a spiritual commonwealth; as such, it possesses a common wealth made up of Christ's super-abundant merits plus those gained by his holy mother and his multitudinous martyrs and saints down the centuries.

This common wealth constitutes the Church's treasury of merits, the so-called *thesaurus Ecclesiae*. From this treasury we may draw vicarious merits – and apply them to the holy souls. By so doing we bring about the remission of at least some of the purgatorial penalties still outstanding on their sins.

Such a let-off from purgatorial punishment is called an indulgence. And by gaining these for the benefit of the souls in purgatory, we help very substantially towards their relief and solace. If partial, an indulgence remits a portion of some holy soul's purgatorial penalties; if plenary, it remits them all, amnesty-wise, thus delivering a soul from its penitential prison and transferring it to God's heavenly kingdom.

Mother Mary and Mother Church

By encouraging us at Medjugorje to become more purgatory-minded, the mother of the Church is simply expressing the compassion and zeal felt by the Church itself towards those helpless multitudes being purified in the flames of God's justice and holiness. Thus the Church has prescribed that a commemoration of the dead be made in each and every Mass. Also, the Church observes an annual All Souls' Day (2 November); on it, priests are authorised to celebrate three Masses for the faithful departed, while extra facilities are granted for the gaining of plenary indulgences.

Furthermore, the Church has dedicated the entire month of November to the souls in purgatory, thereby encouraging us to step up our spiritual alms-giving for their benefit.

The visionary Mirjana has thrown an interesting sidelight on the liberation of holy souls and their transfer to heaven. She reaffirmed in her Jan Connell interview (and here, as always, we bear in mind the norms set out in the introductory chapter) that, according to the mother of God, more souls are freed from purgatory on Christmas Day than is the case on the feast of All Souls (2 November).

Thereupon these newly-beatified citizens of heaven will become so many fresh intercessors on our behalf, especially if we have helped to bring about their release – as Our Lady exhorted us in one of her messages (6 November 1986).

But let us recall that the holy souls can intercede for us no less while still being readied for heaven in purgatory's cleansing torments. Indeed, their prayers are most effective, and we are encouraged to cultivate a special devotion to them. Among others, many saints have done this. For example, St Catherine of Bologna claimed that whatever favour she asked through the holy souls was granted immediately. St John Vianney, too, placed great reliance on the power of their intercession.

Medjugorje and purgatory

No intention recommended to the prayers of the holy souls could be more practical and important than that they help us to practise the Medjugorje message faithfully and generously. For they practise it themselves to a wonderful degree.

In the first place, who is more turned towards God and away from sin than they are, amidst those awesome flames of expiation and purgation? Secondly, their faith is strong and ardent, making them vividly aware of God's kingdom and burningly desirous of seeing him and possessing him everlastingly. As for the third constituent of the Medjugorje message – prayer – it is purgatory's very breath and heartbeat. Fervently and unceasingly the holy souls pray, now adoring God, now renewing their contrition for sin, now offering him their sufferings as due expiation, now interceding with him on our behalf, now thanking him for all his benefits, now communing with the gracious Queen of Purgatory.

The fourth element – penance – lies at the very heart of the purgatory matter. For its inmates live for nothing else than to render to the all-holy Godhead reparation – satisfying, sanctifying reparation – as amends for misdeeds that offended him and defaced themselves.

Throughout the intense spiritual drama of faith, prayer and penance being played out continuously in the midst of fires that crucify human spirits in order to purify them, God's captive debtors enjoy a deep and abiding peace. It is the peace of God that surpasses all human understanding. It is the peace announced by the Bethlehem angels. It is the peace of the Blessed Sacrament. It is the peace of Medjugorje, brought there by Gospa, the Queen of Peace.

Closing prayer to Gospa

We thank you, Mother Mary, for lifting up our eyes to the holy world of purgatory, and for stirring our compassion and zeal towards your many children imprisoned in its purifying flames.

Strengthen our belief in purgatory, O Medjugorje Gospa, that it may became for us a vivid reality and a constant spur to prayer and penance. Teach us to view and use this present world as an outpost of purgatory, offering our crosses and mortifications as advance payment on the debt of expiation owing to God's justice on account of our transgressions.

Sweet and gracious Queen of Purgatory, teach us to be generous in offering suffrages and gaining indulgences, especially plenary ones, on behalf of the suffering penitents. May they be speedily released from their captivity and so come to join you, together with all the angels and saints, in the enjoyment of that Vision which is beatific and everlasting.

10

The Mystery of Hell

It is in the Litany of Loreto that many of Mary's best-loved titles are to be found; there they cluster and sparkle as on a necklace of praise and prayer. One of these titles has a particular relevance in our present context, namely, "Mother of our Saviour". For Medjugorje is very much to do with the salvation wrought by our Saviour; thus, as we shall be seeing, one of the themes highlighted there is heaven.

By the same token, however, those evils from which the Saviour has liberated us – sin and its eternal punishment – are equally featured in Our Lady of Medjugorje's syllabus of lessons.

Without flinching from what Pius XII termed "the frightening aspects of divine revelation", the Medjugorje Madonna sternly warns us, as her Son does in the gospel, that everlasting damnation is a reality confronting every wayfarer within this world of time and probation. She reminds us, in St Francis de Sales' words, that "we are walking in this world between paradise and hell, and that our last step will place us in an everlasting dwelling. To make that last step well, we must try to make all the others well".

So the Medjugorje Madonna, as befits her role as Queen of Prophets, is here inviting us to think about the unthinkable. For that is what hell is – an awesome mystery of human malice, final impenitence, and banishment from God "in the everlasting fire prepared for the devil and his angels" (Mt 25:41).

A key mystery

To underline how integral hell is to her Medjugorje teaching, Our Lady brought it about that four of the visionaries were given a "hellscape" – that is, a vision of that dread reality. Here she followed the same procedure as with the three shepherd children of Fatima, letting them realise the sheer horror of hell and stirring their zeal to offer prayers and sacrifices for dying sinners.

We shall presently consider some of the impressions gained by the visionaries from that experience. But let us first note that our Medjugorje mother, who has made faith a vital element of her basic message, is focusing our minds and hearts on a truth deeply rooted in traditional Catholic teaching. So, before going any further, let us see briefly what the Church tells us about this central, albeit sombre, mystery of perpetual damnation.

The ABC of hell

Hell is a place and state of eternal punishment for serious and unrepented sins. "Those who have done evil", declares the Athanasian Creed, "will go into eternal fire."

The same truth was reaffirmed in the Dogmatic Constitution of Benedict XII: "The souls of those who die in personal grievous sin descend immediately into hell, where they will be tormented by the pains of hell."

Of these pains, first and foremost is the so-called pain of loss. This means that the damned are deprived for all eternity of the vision and possession of God – the infinite source of everything that makes for beatitude.

The secondary punishment of hell is referred to as the pain of sense. This consists in the infliction of positive punishment through an external reality going under the name of fire; it is of the physical order but unlike any earthly fire. We are allowed to believe, though, that fire is here to be taken in a purely metaphorical sense; that is, as symbolic of spiritual pains, notably the torments of conscience. But a good many theologians, both ancient and modern, hold to the view that it is a physical reality.

The number of lost is unknown. Nor has the loss of any given individual been revealed. After the Last Judgment, the bodies of the damned will share in the punishment of their companion souls; which punishment will endure without mitigation and without end.

What Christ taught

What Our Lady teaches us in Medjugorje about hell chimes in

exactly with the Church's doctrine. And this doctrine, in turn, has its roots in Scripture, especially Our Lord's clear-cut teaching in the gospel.

He warns unrepentant sinners – unequivocally, uncompromisingly, repeatedly – about the divine retribution that awaits them in the undying fires of Gehenna. Here he applies to hell the name of a ravine to the south-west of Jerusalem that was used as a garbage-dump; formerly it had been infamous as a sanctuary of Moloch where, moreover, human sacrifices had been offered.

Thus the Saviour speaks in warning terms of "the unquenchable fire of hell; the worm that eats them there never dies; the fire is never extinguished" (Mt 9:44). In asking people to follow him and to believe his gospel, he emphasises that their eternal salvation is at stake; that if they die in their sins they will merit eternal punishment. Thus, each time under the penalty of hell, he warns them of the sin against the Holy Spirit (Mt 12:32), the sin of scandal (Mt 18:8), the sin of uncharitableness (Mt 5:32). While the kingdom of heaven is for those who do his Father's will, the penalty of hell awaits all "workers of iniquity" (Mt 7:21-23).

Many of Our Lord's parables end with the condemnation of the wicked to hell. Examples of this are: the chaff and the wheat (Mt 13:24-30); the net full of fish (Mt 13:47-50); Dives and Lazarus (Lk 16:18-31); the great supper (Lk 14:16-24); the royal wedding feast (Mt 22:1-14); the wise and foolish virgins (Mt 25:1-13); the talents (Mt 25:14-30).

Again, Our Lord likened our way through this world to one of two roads leading respectively to life or perdition (Lk 7:13-14). And he expressly enjoined us "to fear him who can destroy both body and soul in hell" (Mt 10:28).

But surely the most impressive warning of all are those terrible words of malediction due to be pronounced upon the reprobate by the Christ of Judgment Day: "Depart from me, you cursed, into the everlasting fire, which was prepared for the devil and his angels" (Mt 25:41).

To deny the doctrine of hell, then, is to deny the gospel of Christ – and, in so doing, the Christ of the gospel.

A vista of hell

On 5 November 1981, four of the Medjugorje visionaries (Vicka, Marija, Ivan and Jakov) were allowed by Our Lady to see something of hell. The remaining two (Mirjana and Ivanka) had expressed a disinclination to behold so horrifying a spectacle.

The mother of God said that her purpose in giving the visionaries a vista of the gehennal world was to impress upon them the dreadful punishment awaiting sinners who wilfully reject her Son's redeeming love and leave this world in that state. She added that we should pray and make sacrifices for those dying in a state of serious sin.

Some two weeks after that initial experience, Vicka and Jakov were given a more extended view of the place and state of eternal reprobation and torment. Again the mother of our Saviour urged them to be generous with prayers and sacrifices on behalf of dying sinners.

What the four visionaries tell us about hell tallies to a remarkable degree with what mystics down the centuries have reported of a similar experience. Of course, we must make due allowance in all such mystical experiences for elements of symbolism and relativism adapted to the psychology of those undergoing them. For, by definition, extra-terrestrial realities and conditions are beyond our ken. This is not to imply, however, that a visionary's experience lacks all objective value.

The visionaries testify

Vicka has painted a fairly detailed picture of the hellscape she witnessed on two occasions. We find it in the excellent interview with Jan Connell. Supplementary material is supplied in her account of the experience she made to Fr Janka Bubalo. "In hell's centre", reports Vicka, "is a huge fire, like a sea of raging flames. Before people go into the fire they appear normal. The more they are against God's will, the deeper they enter the fire. And, the deeper they go, the more they rage against God. When they emerge from the fire, they no longer have human shapes. They look more like grotesque animals, but unlike any on earth. They are horrible, ugly, angry. When they came out of the fire they raged and smashed everything around them, hissing, gnashing and screeching." Vicka added that demons torture and torment the damned, who mouth fearful blasphemies and obscenities.

Marija's testimony is very similar. "Hell", she says, "is a sea of fire with blackened figures moving about it." She particularly noticed among the lost a beautiful girl who, on emerging from the flames, looked like a wild, repulsive animal.

Our Lady's words to the visionaries were: "This is the punishment for those who do not love God. Many today go to hell." Vicka reports further: "The Blessed Mother says that the people in hell are there because they choose to go there. It is their choice when they die. It is their will that they go to hell."

Marija testifies in similar vein. "Anyone who goes to hell", she quotes the mother of God as saying, "does so because they choose it. God does not condemn anyone. They condemn themselves."

Parallel testimonies
What the Medjugorje visionaries report about hell parallels in many points the testimonies of others who have had a similar experience.

St Lydwine was shown the abode of the damned by her guardian angel. But she could not bear the sight of the flames and the torments. Still less could she endure the shouts of rage and despair mixing with the blasphemies. St Frances of Rome reacted in much the same way. Later the very mention of hell would fill her with horror at the nightmare memory of gehennal flames, animal-like figures, and an unholy bedlam of blasphemy and bitter hate.

As for St Teresa of Avila, so horrified was she by her vision of hell that, even after an interval of six years, she "still felt chilled with fear at the very thought of it". And she summed up the mystery of hell – its furious fires, its animalised humans, its cacophony of curses and blasphemies – in the words: "It is a place without God."

Few mystics have been given so profound an experience of the gehennal world as the Spanish religious, Sister Josefa Menendez.

She, too, recorded its punishing flames and awful sights and sounds. But she repeatedly dwelt on the greatest torment of hell, namely, the soul's inability to love. One of the damned was heard to cry out: "This is my torture: that I want to love but cannot. There is nothing left for me but hatred and despair. We are not able to love him whom we are now bound to hate. We hunger for love; we are consumed with desire for it. But it is too late."

One of the Fatima visionaries, who is better known to us as Sister Lucia, now an ageing Carmelite in Coimbra, wrote at the request of her bishop the following account of the hell-experience she and her two companions had in 1917: "We saw as it were a sea of fire. Plunged in this fire were demons and souls in human form, like transparent burning embers, all blackened and burnished bronze, floating about in the conflagration, amid shrieks and groans of pain and despair, which horrified us and made us tremble with fear. It must have been this sight which caused me to cry out, as people say who heard me."

The pain of loss

As was noted a little earlier, St Teresa of Avila encapsulated the whole meaning of hell in the phrase: "It is a place without God."

It is accepted Church teaching (implicitly defined by Benedict XII and the Fourth Lateran Council) that eternal punishment consists primarily and principally in the pain of loss – banishment for ever from the Beatific Vision and the possession and enjoyment of God going with it.

Our Lady made it clear to the Medjugorje visionaries that those who leave this world with personal, grave, unrepented guilt on their conscience themselves make the choice of eternal loss. That is, their choice becomes eternalised; it is the logical and fixed-state consequence of their aversion from God. And their experience of banishment and loss corresponds to their degree of aversion from God.

So what the lost inflict upon themselves is equivalently auto-damnation without end "in Satan's prison" (Rv 20:3,7). Wilfully and disastrously they choose self-banishment and self-exile from the God of eternal life, and thus "incur Satan's doom" (1 Tm 3:6). Hence the maledictory verdict pronounced by the Christ of Judgment Day will merely ratify the self-damnation already declared upon themselves by the outcasts: "Depart from me, you cursed, into the everlasting fire, which was prepared for the devil and his angels" (Mt 25:41).

The second death

"The perpetual death of the damned, that is, their separation from the life of God, will go on without end and be their common lot." Here St Augustine was referring to the pain of loss as described by St John the Evangelist: "The second death in the lake of fire" (Rv 20:4).

As distinct from the first or biological death, namely, the separation of soul from body, the second or eschatological death denotes the separation of a soul from its Creator and Last End.

It is this sense of loss, with its accompanying frustration and despair, which constitutes the worst torment suffered by the wicked. For it was their destiny to behold and find everlasting beatitude in the Infinite Being who alone, as Pascal says, can fill that abyss which is the human heart. But hell is the living and unending death of that destiny. Now these tormented souls have separated themselves for ever from the divine infinitude of truth, goodness, beauty, love and peace – those very things for which their human hearts hunger and yearn.

Hell, then, is the City of the Second Death. It is perpetually God-forsaken because it is peopled by those who have perpetually forsaken God. Fugitives from divine love, they are beyond all repentance and every remedy. Their time of elective freedom having expired when they departed this life, their wills are irreversibly fixed in that fatal final choice they made at the moment of death.

Those suffering the pain of loss have sundered themselves contumaciously from the light of divine life and now find themselves doomed forever in the "exterior darkness" (Mt 8:12). As for the remorse, the bitterness, the despair they experience in realising that they have forfeited eternally the vision and possession of God, this is what Our Lord meant when he spoke about "the worm that never dies" (Mt 9:44).

The pain of sense

In that nightmare scenario of hell witnessed by themselves, the Medjugorje visionaries observed, among other things, that its fires not only inflicted torment upon the wicked but seemed somehow to detain and imprison them as well.

This observation happens to tally with what St Thomas and many other theologians teach about hell's secondary punitive factor – its so-called pain of sense. This, they hold, is not purely subjective and metaphorical; rather, it is pain inflicted by an objective, external agency akin to fire, which is of a wholly different species, however, from the terrestrial kind we are familiar with.

A further function of this gehennal fire, they also teach, is to act as a barrier or wall restricting the movements of the inmates. Mystical writers amply corroborate this teaching. For example, St Ignatius describes the souls of the lost as being enveloped and constricted by fiery bodies. And St Teresa of Avila saw the damned as it were hemmed in by walls of fire.

After the General Judgment, the bodies of those condemned to the second death will share in the souls' fate and accordingly suffer the pain of sense because of sins committed.

The punishment of hell is not equal for everyone. Its degree corresponds to the sinner's aversion from God and conversion to creatures. Here we can reflect that sin represents the very antithesis of the Medjugorje message's primary item (conversion to God and aversion from what hinders this), while hell is its eternal vindication and sanction.

Fear of the Lord

Our Lady of Medjugorje instructs us in her messages to ask the Holy Spirit for an increase of his sevenfold gifts. One of these is most relevant to our context: fear of the Lord. It was equivalently invoked by the Lord's mother herself when she said to the four visionaries after showing them something of what damnation entails: "This is the punishment of those who do not love God. Many today go to hell."

Our Lord was most explicit about it. "Fear him", he warned us, "who can destroy both body and soul in hell" (Mt 10:28). This warning is echoed by the author of the Imitation of Christ. "It is a good thing," he says, "that if the love of God does not reclaim us from evil, at least the fear of hell will restrain us." And that it does, in fact, have power to restrain us from evil was recognised by Pascal when he wrote: "It is fear of hell that peoples heaven."

So it is altogether a most salutary and much-needed lesson we are here receiving from the Medjugorje Madonna. Karl Rahner's words will help us to appreciate it all the more. "The purpose of the doctrine of hell", he writes, "is not to provide abstract data or to satisfy our curiosity, but to bring us to our senses and conversion. The dogma of hell means that human life is threatened by the real possibility of human shipwreck, because man freely disposes of himself and can therefore freely refuse himself to God."

Nobody faces up to the threat of eternal shipwreck more realistically and humbly than the saints. "Give me thy grace, good God," Thomas More prayed, "to foresee and consider the everlasting fires of hell." St Francis Borgia did exactly that every single day. So did St Francis Xavier, St Teresa of Avila and the Curé d'Ars, to name but a few.

A warning for everyone

All this serves to illustrate a further point, which is also alluded to by Our Lady in her Medjugorje instructions; namely, it is precisely those who are more endowed with God's gifts, be they of the natural or supernatural kind, that stand most in need of these warning reminders about the danger of losing one's soul. So seriously did St Benedict take it that he recommended his monks, in their fourth rule, to keep constantly alive within themselves "the dread of hell".

Fear of the Lord enables us to see, as it did St Paul, that "there is graciousness in God, and there is also severity" (Rm 11:12). The same gift of the Holy Spirit further made him realistic enough to recognise the peril overhanging his own salvation, let alone that of his converts. "I buffet my own body," he said, "and make it my slave; or I, who have preached to others, may myself be rejected as worthless" (1 Co 9:27).

So the Mother of our Saviour is solicitously admonishing us, one and all, that "he who thinks he stands firmly should beware of a fall" (1 Co 10:12); or, in St Bernard's phrase, "no security is too great when eternity is at stake." The Curé d'Ars summed it all up when he said: "He who really fears hell will not fall into it."

Mirjana's problems
In her thoughtful and forthright way, the visionary Mirjana has voiced problems that have puzzled many minds down the centuries. In a recorded interview with Fr Svetozar Kraljevic (10 January 1983), she related how, during an apparition, she asked the mother of God to explain some points about hell that caused her difficulties.

The text goes: "I asked her how God could be so unmerciful as to throw people into hell to suffer forever. Here in our world, if a person commits a crime and goes to jail, he stays there for a while and is then forgiven. So why do they stay in hell forever?

"Our Lady replied that souls who go to hell have stopped thinking favourably of God and now curse him more and more. So they have already become a part of hell and choose not to be delivered from it.

"I next asked her if people who go to hell don't pray for their salvation. Could God be so unmerciful as not to hear their prayers? The Madonna then explained it to me, saying that people who go to hell do not pray at all; instead, they blame God for everything. In effect, they become one with hell and get used to it. They rage against God, and they suffer. But they always refuse to pray to God. In hell they hate him ever more and more."

Hell's eternity
This serves to confirm what we have already been seeing. Those who die impenitent no longer enjoy elective freedom with regard

139

to their last end but remain fixed unalterably and bitterly in their anti-God state of mind. In Our Lady's words, "they become one with hell and get used to it". Beyond all repentance and prayer, they eternalise the state of auto-damnation they wilfully chose for themselves on leaving this world.

Thus the Church's conciliar teaching is that the fate of such people is "everlasting punishment, eternal damnation". Like the demons with whom they share their infernal abode, they are totally cut off from the Holy Spirit, explains St Basil; hence there is no possible movement of grace leading to prayer and repentance.

We have also seen that, throughout all Scripture, the future destiny of humanity is unfailingly presented in terms of eternal life or eternal loss. Already in the fourth century, the theory according to which both the angelic and human inmates of hell will be restored to God's friendship was officially condemned by the Church. The "eternal darkness" (Jude 13) of the Gehennal City will not ever – because it cannot – see the light of a new dawn.

Countering false views

Nothing could be more needed and opportune than that the Queen of Prophets should be using Medjugorje to re-affirm, for the benefit of this unbelieving and sinful generation, the reality of eternal punishment.

Many people nowadays are in a state of doubt and confusion about the issue. Some modern theologians have set out to demythologise hell, rejecting the Church's traditional doctrine as a grave aberration unworthy of the merciful Saviour. They further accuse the traditional doctrine of portraying God as vengeful and vindictive. And they end up by dismissing the whole concept of eternal damnation as a barbarous Gothic fantasy rooted in fundamentalism of the most primitive kind.

Views such as these, apart from contradicting the Church's infallible teaching and therefore being heretical, violate two fundamental principles that supply the very key to hell's mystery. The first is God's infinite holiness and justice. The second is the tremendous dignity and responsibility that go with being a human person.

Two principles

Sin's whole point, let us remember, is that it is an offence against God. And when we reflect, as St Ignatius bids us, on "who God is against whom we sin", we gain an insight into sin's terrible evil. For God is our Creator and Lord, infinite in his power, holiness, justice, wisdom and other perfections. Therefore, wilful grave offences against his holiness and justice partake in some sort, St Thomas teaches, of his own infinity, and accordingly deserve an eternity of punishment.

Equally indispensable for the light it throws on hell is the immense dignity and responsibility belonging to every human being without exception. This truth shines out with great power and clarity from Our Lord's solemn declaration: "What does it profit a man if he gains the whole world, yet suffers the loss of his own soul?" (Mk 8:36).

In other words, our whole meaning and value as human persons is that, being rational and self-determining, we choose for ourselves which of the alternative destinies – salvation or damnation – will be ours throughout eternity. This explains why Vicka, instructed by Our Lady, could say of the impenitent sinners she beheld in the gehennal fires: "It's their own fault. The choice was theirs. God loves everyone – but they decided to go to hell". Marija bore similar testimony. "Anyone who goes to hell," she said, "does so because they choose it."

Every soul is great

"Man's life", said Chesterton, "is planned on a scale colossal. I tell you: every soul is great." Now what constitutes our greatness is precisely this factor we are here considering. We are rational beings, free agents, self-determining individuals. In a word, we are living images of God.

Throughout our lives we make multiple choices between good

141

and evil. It is the ultimate choice we make at death that is so momentous, since it determines which of the two eternities – heaven or hell – will be our final abode. To quote St Francis de Sales' words once again: "We are walking in this world between paradise and hell, and that last step will place us in an everlasting dwelling."

Truly, therefore, "man's life is planned on a scale colossal – and every soul is great." For we have been endowed with the titanic power – and responsibility – of deciding either for God and his heavenly kingdom or for that Godless and anti-God desolation we call hell. This awesome moment of truth and decision confronts each one of us when death brings us to the crossroads of time and eternity.

St Bernard was quite clear that we are the arbiters of our own destinies. "Take away self-will," he said, "and there would be no hell." Or as St Augustine put it: "God simply permits the sinner to have his own way." The plain and terrible truth is that, in the words of St Ambrose, "those who perish do so by their own negligence".

Upholding truth

Not for sentimental reasons, then, nor on grounds of a false humanitarianism, should one dilute, still less deny, the dogma of perpetual damnation. In accepting it, we are not making God out to be a cruel tyrant; rather, we are respecting his infinite holiness and justice. In addition, we are being faithful to his crystal-clear teaching in the Gospel. Furthermore, in accepting this dogma we are honouring – as God does – our noble prerogative of personal freedom, which includes our freedom to choose for ourselves between the two eternities.

All this comes across very loud and clear in Medjugorje. For the Mother of our Saviour sees how urgently it is needed by today's Church and world. She also sees, very clearly, the truth of the old adage: religions, like bees, die if you remove their sting.

Closing prayer to Gospa

We thank you, Queen of Prophets, for bringing to our attention at Medjugorje the mystery of hell. Help us to understand it more deeply so that we may avoid all sin and finally attain to the glory of heaven.

Win for us, O Spouse of the Holy Spirit, an increased measure of his precious gift of fearing the Lord. So may we truly fear him who can destroy both body and soul in hell. And through this filial fear may we be led to that wisdom and charity which flow from it.

Mother of Jesus Crucified, inspire us, as you did the Medjugorje visionaries, to appreciate that his sufferings were undergone to free us from sin in this world and eternal damnation in the next.

Fill us, Gospa of Medjugorje, Queen of Apostles, with a burning zeal for souls. And may we be instrumental in helping many, especially through our prayers and sacrifices, to reach eternal life.

11

Vestibule of Heaven

"Because you have such a glorious goal set before you, I am reminding you of it again and again" (2 P 1:12). This text aptly applies to one of the Queen of Heaven's key concerns in Medjugorje. She emphasises the reality of heaven and its all-importance as our eternal destiny; and, at the same time, she guides us there with solicitous care and much love.

Nor should we be surprised at this. Just as our eternal salvation is "the aim and quest of the prophets" (1 P 1:5), it is no less that of the Queen of Prophets. And, in her further Medjugorje role as Queen of Peace, she often lifts our gaze to that eternal city whose very name signifies "vision of peace" – the New Jerusalem, the City of God.

Moreover, she walks alongside us as a loving mother and sure guide on our lifelong pilgrimage. Her message of 25 May 1991 says all this and more: "I am ever at your side to provide help and guidance, dear children, on your way to heaven. There is to be found that joy through which, already now, you can live the life of heaven in this world."

Messenger from heaven

Presently we shall be considering a selection of Mary's other messages about heaven. Beforehand, however, let us note that Medjugorje's first and foremost message is the Messenger herself. Besides bringing us wisdom and counsel from on high, she literally embodies heavenly realities and presents them in our midst.

For Mary's glorified human self is caught up into that sublime experience known as the Beatific Vision. And her glorified humanity already shares in the radiance and perpetual youth of the risen life. Thus she is described by the visionaries as a wonderfully beautiful girl in her late teens – a far cry from the septuagenarian that God's mother would have been, we may reasonably surmise –

basing ourselves on the legend, widespread in both Eastern and Western devotional literature, that Our Lady lived some twenty or so years after her Son's resurrection – when her own earthly days reached their end.

Another heavenly reality commonly brought to our attention by the Medjugorje Madonna is the angelic world. She frequently appears with an escort of angels, who are heaven's first citizens and honour her as their queen.

Messages about heaven

Here are some selected messages from the Queen of Heaven on what is clearly one of her favourite themes:

● "Dear children, I am your mother, and for this reason desire to lead each one of you to holiness in all its completeness. For I want every one of you both to be happy here on earth and in due course to be with me in heaven. This is not only my desire but my whole purpose in coming here to Medjugorje" (25 May 1987).

● "Dear children, I love you with a special love and wish to lead all of you to God in heaven. What I want you to realise is that this life lasts but a short while compared with that of heaven. So commit yourselves to God anew today. Only in this way can I bring home to you how dear you are to me and how much I want all of you to be saved and to be with me in heaven" (27 November 1986).

● "Never forget, dear children, that your life is as transitory as a springtime blossom. Your witness will have value not only for your present life but for all eternity" (25 March 1988).

● "It is my desire, dear children, that every one of you who has been in or near this fountain of grace which is Medjugorje will reach heaven, thanks to the special gift which you will give me, namely holiness. Therefore pray, and direct your lives towards holiness" (13 November 1986).

● "Please cooperate with me so that I can offer you to God and guide you on the path of salvation" (25 June 1987).

● "Pay no attention to unimportant things but make heaven your goal" (25 July 1987).

● "You know that I love you, dear children, and have come here out of love, so that I could show you the path to peace and the salvation of your souls. Give witness through your lives. Sacrifice them for the salvation of the world...In heaven you will receive the Father's promised reward" (25 February 1988).

● "For myself I want nothing. Everything is ordered towards the salvation of your souls" (25 October 1988).

Visionaries shown heaven
On the feast of All Saints, 1981, all the visionaries (except Ivan) were given by Our Lady a vista of heaven. And Vicka, who reports this in her Notebook, adds that they found it "a region of great light and happiness, indescribably beautiful, and full of human beings and angels". Ivanka recognised among the human throng her mother and another woman she had known.

A fortnight later, Vicka and Jakov were privileged by the mother of God with a more extended showing of heaven. "We spent about twenty minutes there," Vicka has recorded. "Heaven is a vast space, and everything is bathed in a wonderful light. The people you see there, the angels, the flowers – wonderful peace fills everything. From their faces you can see that the people there are very happy. Our Lady said to us: 'See how happy, how full of joy, is everyone in heaven!' "

From sundry interviews (notably Jan Connell's excellent *Queen of the Cosmos)* we learn something about the impressions gained by the other visionaries from their vision of heaven. These impressions must be read in the light of the guidelines given in the introductory chapter.

"I saw it," Ivanka relates, "as in a picture. It is very, very beautiful. Everyone I saw was filled with happiness. I cannot explain it – nor can I forget. I myself experience something of that happiness when I am with Our Lady – and when I pray."

Mirjana gave this account of her experience. "I saw heaven as if in a movie. Yes, it is an actual place. But the trees, the meadows and the sky are totally different from anything we know on earth. And the light is much more brilliant. Heaven is beautiful beyond anything I know of in this world. The first thing I noticed was the faces of the people; they were radiating a kind of inner light, which showed how immensely happy they were. The people were walking in a beautiful park. They have everything in heaven. They neither need anything nor want anything. They are totally satisfied."

Marija reported as follows: "I had a vision of heaven. It was like watching a movie or looking out of a window. I saw a multitude of people and lots of flowers. The people were full of joy; all of them were giving thanks to God for his gifts. They realise how much love God has for them."

Ivan limited himself to giving a reflection on his experience rather than an account of it. "Heaven is worth any cost," he said. "Jesus showed us that with his death on the cross. The people in heaven are happy. They live in the fullness of God."

Medjugorje mirrors heaven
What the visionaries experienced of heaven overwhelmed them with its happiness, holiness, peace, fullness of life, and beauty. Valid and objective though their witness is, yet it fails to convey anything above a watered-down, relative and symbolic idea of heaven's reality, for reasons we shall shortly be considering.

But let us first reflect on the fact that "this fountain of grace" which is Medjugorje strikes many pilgrims as being a very vestibule of heaven, affording them a glimpse into their eternal homeland, so unique is its atmosphere of peace, prayer, holiness and joy. Indeed, they would apply to Medjugorje what St

Bernadette said of her beloved Lourdes: "It is my heaven on earth."

This explains why pilgrims feel sad on leaving Medjugorje, and think back on it with nostalgia, which literally means "longing for home". For Medjugorje has become their spiritual home, their heaven on earth. Through it their faith, hope and love become focused, as never before, on that glorious City of God to which Mary beckons us so invitingly, calling us, her children, like the true mother she is, to our eternal home.

Everyone is a pilgrim

Through Medjugorje in general, and through pilgrimages there in particular, the Queen of Heaven is reminding this earthbound generation that, for every single human being without exception, life is a pilgrimage through time to eternity. In this world we are all "pilgrims and strangers" (1 P 2:11). Our human situation is that "we have an everlasting city but not here; our goal is the city that is one day to be" (Heb 13:14).

God, in other words, has so made us that heaven is our heart's homeland. For heaven really means the possession and enjoyment of God, who is in himself infinite truth, goodness, and beauty – those very things for which our hearts hunger but can never adequately attain, let alone retain, in this fickle, passing world.

"I feel in my heart," wrote St Therese of Lisieux, "desires that are infinite." Similarly St Augustine declares that the human heart is so made that its restless quest can be quieted only in God, the infinite and loving fountainhead of all perfections.

Every human being, then, little though he or she may realise it, is a pilgrim in search of the Absolute. For of its very nature the human heart is on pilgrimage to him who alone can slake its thirst for unlimited and unending truth, goodness and beauty.

Meanwhile, of course, the human heart is under pressure from false gods to follow forbidden paths that lead to ultimate frustration and ruin. In that tragic event, the pilgrim ends up as a vagabond, perpetually excluded from the Land of Desires.

148

Chaucer's verse serves both as warning and encouragement:

> Here is no home; here is but wilderness.
> Forth, pilgrim, forth! Forth, beast, out of thy stall!
> Know thy country; look up; thank God of all.

What heaven essentially is

Chesterton once remarked playfully that it is more important to get your head into heaven than heaven into your head. This is quite right, of course. At the same time, though, faith ever seeks a clearer understanding of what its formulas profess. And we have been encouraged in this direction by the Medjugorje Madonna's particular devotion to the Creed as her "favourite prayer".

What, then, does the Creed itself say about heaven? The answer is found in its two concluding articles: "I look forward to the resurrection of the body and the life of the world to come."

This precise and unadorned formula brings to mind Newman's comment: "Neither Scripture nor theology provides sufficient light for an exact picture of life after death." Indeed, in a well-known text, Scripture admits its own inadequacy to depict the after-life: "The eye has not seen, nor ear heard, nor has it entered into the heart of man, what things God has prepared for those who love him" (1 Co 2:9; cf. Is 64:4).

Hopelessly inadequate, too, is the testimony of the Medjugorje visionaries, as is that of others who have had mystical experience of heaven. The reason is that heaven's central reality is something out of this world, in every sense. We call it the Beatific Vision. Our glorified faculties, having been endowed with a specific "light of glory" rendering them capable of the experience, will actually behold God as he is – the infinitely perfect triune God – face to face (cf. 1 Jn 3:2; 1 Co 13:12).

From this intuitive knowledge of God flows an immense joy and happiness. In addition to this there is so-called "accessory happiness"; it derives from other heavenly possessions that will be ours along with God. Included among these is the company and mutual love of the glorified Christ, the Queen of Heaven, the angels and the saints, as well as an understanding of the wonders of creation.

Our Lord, in speaking about his Father's many-mansioned dwelling-place, referred to the degrees of heavenly reward that will be apportioned to the blessed in accordance with their merits. Each will see, possess and enjoy God to the fullness of their glorified faculties. St Augustine suggests a useful comparison in this connection. Consider, he says, the following range of containers – a thimble, a cup, a jug, a barrel, a pool, a lake, a sea, an ocean. Diverse though their capacities are, each attains its maximum when filled up.

Adventure into the infinite
Heaven will be an exciting, non-stop adventure of our minds and hearts into the unsearchable mysteries of the Godhead. For it is in knowing God that eternal life essentially consists (cf. Jn 17:3). But we shall never know him fully, totally, exhaustively. That is what is understood by divine incomprehensibility.

God, though eminently knowable, cannot ever be completely known by any created intellect, even the most elevated angelic one. What this in effect means is that in heaven there could never possibly be anything akin to staleness, monotony, weariness or boredom. So we shall never feel inclined to cast God aside like yesterday's newspaper or a solved crossword puzzle.

On the contrary, our intellects, illumined powerfully by the light of glory given as the indispensable medium of knowledge in heaven, will penetrate ever-deeper into the mysteries of God's life. Indeed, so infinitely rich and endless is the revelation of those mysteries that a great Christian theologian, Origen, described the heaven-experience as "an eternal gospel". For it will amount to an everlasting discovery of further truths and deeper depths and undreamed-of vistas as our glorified selves pursue their exciting adventure into the God of surprises.

It is consoling to reflect that the Queen of Heaven, who has been beholding the Beatific Vision for nearly twenty centuries now in terms of terrestrial time, will during this while surely have

150

drawn untold riches from the infinitude of that "eternal gospel"; these are now numbered among the truths she treasures and ponders in her Immaculate Heart (cf. Lk 2:17).

Life in heaven

One very substantial joy God has in store for us is the company of the Queen of Heaven, his mother and ours. The same applies to the angels, particularly our own guardian, and all the saints, especially our patrons.

Moreover, we shall be reunited in heaven with all our own dear dead ones. Mourning them, we say with Tennyson: "Oh for the touch of a vanished hand, and the sound of a voice that is still!" But, thank God, reunion with them lies ahead in heaven, where we shall say goodbye, forever, to all goodbyes.

We shall likewise say goodbye in heaven to things like sickness and sorrow, privation and suffering, distress and heartache. In the words of the beloved disciple, who during his exile in Patmos was given a glimpse of paradisal realities: "God will wipe away every tear from their eyes, and there will be no more death, or mourning, or cries of distress, no more sorrow; those old things have passed away" (Rv 21:4).

What will also pass away is something all of us are all-too-familiar with in this world – time. In God's heavenly kingdom we shall somehow participate in his eternal duration. So we shall no longer be subject to those sad things inherent and inevitable in a world of clocks and calendars, and therefore of change and decay: ageing, infirmity, death, the grave, the crematorium.

The risen mother of God

"The resurrection of the body and life everlasting" – the credal formula relating to our future heavenly status is already embodied and exemplified in the person of Mary Immaculate. As the preface for the Assumption states: "Mary was taken up body and soul into heaven to be the beginning and pattern of the Church in its perfection, and a sign of hope and comfort for God's people on their pilgrim way."

151

The Medjugorje visionaries testify to the Queen of Heaven's radiantly beautiful and youthful appearance. Hereby she is demonstrating that her own glorified humanity is a prototype, an exemplar, of what our own will become when the dead rise on Judgment Day.

So, through her actual apparitions at Medjugorje, let alone her messages, the Saviour's mother is gracing our world with a fresh beacon of faith in the resurrection of the body and, too, with a powerful buttress to our hope of attaining it on that day of days.

Our bodily resurrection

This credal truth has a very strong scriptural backing, not least in St Paul. "Christ", he says, "will form this humbled body of ours anew, moulding it into the image of his own glorified body" (Ph 3:20). And in another key text he affirms that "earth-born man" will be transfigured into "heaven-born man" when his mortal nature is "clothed with immortality and incorruptible life" (1 Co 15:48,52,53).

What this entails is that our earthly bodies will be refashioned and wholly transformed after the pattern of the Risen Saviour's. Like his, then, they will enjoy complete integrity and be free from all distortion, malformation and defects. As St Thomas teaches: "Man will rise again in the greatest possible natural perfection."

From this principle St Thomas goes on to infer that God will restore our risen selves to youthfulness in its prime condition, youthfulness at its peak (to give a free translation of the Angelic Doctor's original phrase: *perfecta aetas juvenilis).

Certainly these qualities shine out in the humanity both of Our Lady and of her Divine Son, as is amply attested by all who have been privileged to be visionaries, including the Medjugorje ones. Identical qualities will shine out in the humanity of all who are "found worthy to attain that other world and resurrection from the dead" (Lk 20:35).

Therefore, no matter how disease, death and its sequel may have ravaged our bodies even to the point of obliteration, they will be raised to a celestial condition by the God of the General Resurrection. And he will bestow upon them, among his other gifts, the golden one of perpetual youth in his paradisal kingdom to come.

Of Eucharist and roses

So integral to Christian faith and hope is the resurrection of the body that Our Lord has linked it closely with his Eucharistic mysteries. And, because these mysteries lie at its very heart, Medjugorje moves us to look forward all the more eagerly to the day when our bodies vibrate with the vitalities and *élan* of our personal resurrection from the dead.

Christ's words are as plain as plain can be. "I myself," he said, "am the living bread that has come down from heaven. If anyone eats of this bread, he shall live for ever...The man who eats my flesh and drinks my blood enjoys eternal life, and I will raise him up at the last day" (Jn 6:51,55).

This link-up between the Eucharist and our bodily resurrection is commonly made by the Church in its liturgy. For example, in the Eucharistic hymn, the *Sacrum Convivium,* faith is professed in the Body of Christ as providing "a pledge of our own future glory".

Yes, the Christ of the Parousia will re-fashion, re-mould these humbled bodies of ours into the form of "heaven-born man, clothed with immortality and incorruptible life" (Ph 3:20; 1 Co 15:53). It all clearly spells transformation, transfiguration, a starlight new order of existence and experience.

Dante had a vivid sense of this consoling mystery. During man's mortal days, he said, he is like a caterpillar; in the grave he goes through the chrysalis stage; and then, wonderfully, he develops at his resurrection into an angel-like butterfly.

Chesterton, too, recognised the sheer wonder of the destiny opened up for us through the Saviour's death and resurrection. "If seeds in the black earth", he wrote, "can grow into such beautiful roses, what will not the heart of man become in his long journey towards the stars?"

153

God's brave new world

St Peter tells us that, when this present world is destroyed by fire, it is destined to be replaced by "a new heaven and a new earth" (2 P 3:13). Thus will be ushered in what Scripture variously refers to as "the regeneration of the world" (Mt 19:28), "the restitution of all things" (Ac 3:21), the setting free of created nature from "the tyranny of corruption, to share in the glorious freedom of God's sons" (Rm 8:21).

So, when God fashions the new heaven and the new earth, filling the entire cosmos with the light of his presence, this present order, this brave old world of ours, will become a fresh creation. And, when our cosmos is restructured, all material creation, which is "full of expectancy as it groans meanwhile in a common travail," will finally share in "the glorious freedom of the sons of God" and duly take on a higher – indeed, a heavenly – quality (Rm 8:19-22).

What this, in effect, means is that the glorified universe will be endowed with paradisal splendour, its whole purpose and function being to provide, for endless ages to come, a worthy dwelling-place for the Word Incarnate and his multitudinous brothers and sisters.

It is the Word Incarnate who will be architect and builder of that Brave New World, our true and eternal fatherland. The pierced hands of the Divine Artisan will bring into being the masterpiece that inspired the Apostle Peter to write: "We are to share an inheritance that is incorruptible, inviolable, unfading. It is stored up for you in heaven. How ineffable your joy will be, and how sublime, when you reap the fruit of that faith of yours" (1 P 1:4,8,9).

Treasury of everlasting joy

We can now see more clearly why Our Lady so highlights heaven in her Medjugorje teaching, and is even on record as saying: "Dear children, I want every one of you to be happy here on earth and in due course to be with me in heaven. This is not only my desire but my whole purpose in coming here to Medjugorje" (25 May 1987).

For heaven is our very destiny. At all costs we must attain to that "treasury of everlasting joy," as Shakespeare calls it. More than being the divinely-appointed Journey's End to life's long marathon, heaven will mark the beginning of our endless and wonderful adventure into God's infinite truth, goodness and beauty. So we must make it our most earnest business to "lay hold of eternal life" (1 Tm 6:12). There is gold in Browning's advice:

> Lose who may – I still can say,
> Those who win heaven, blest are they.

Finally, two considerations will help us to see why heaven is bound to be marvellous beyond all description. St Bernard supplies the first. "If this land of our exile and place of our probation", he asks, "is so exquisite, what must be the beauty and glory of our true home?" St Augustine makes the same point. "If this vale of tears and prison-like exile is so full of goodness and beauty," he reasons, "infinitely more so must be the abode we shall share for endless years with the God of Glory."

The second consideration bears upon the bitter sufferings undergone by Our Lord during his passion. These sufferings were redemptive; that is, they were the price he paid to save us from eternal damnation and to make paradise regainable. That terrible price itself tells us what immense value the Word Incarnate attaches to the prize of paradise.

Closing prayer to Gospa

O glorious Gospa, Queen of Heaven, we thank you for the inspiration you give us in Medjugorje to see heaven as our true home and to aspire after it ardently. Help us to be faithful and generous in practising daily that sure guide through this world to beatitude in the City of God – your Medjugorje message.

Fill us more and more with the spirit of prayer, prayer from the heart, prayer that is entwined around the Rosary, prayer that draws rich nourishment from the Eucharistic mysteries.

155

Gracious Queen of the Angels, pray that we pilgrims on our way to eternal beatitude may be docile to the guardianship and guidance of those blessed spirits who unbrokenly behold the face of our Father in heaven, and whom he, in his solicitous providence, has commanded to keep us in all our ways.

O Queen of All Saints, we look forward with longing to enjoying the Beatific Vision along with you and the entire company of the blessed, especially those who on earth have been near and dear to us. Through their prayers united with yours, loving mother, may we safely reach our true home in the City of God – the New Medjugorje nestling among the eternal hills, the hills of heaven, the hills of home.

Appendix

Guide to Indulgences

As we have seen, an indulgence is a remission of divine penalties attaching to sins, the guilt of which has, of course, been forgiven. Whereas a partial indulgence remits these penalties in part (hence the name), a plenary indulgence remits them in their entirety. All indulgences may be applied to the holy souls. The following norms are taken from the Church's official *Enchiridion of Indulgences* (January 1969).

1. Partial indulgences
● The Church no longer quantifies these, as she formerly did, in terms of days, weeks, months, years, quarantines.

● A partial indulgence happens to attach to *practically every common prayer and devotion in daily usage.* For example, the Our Father, Hail Mary, Glory Be, Memorare, Hail Holy Queen, Guardian Angel Prayer, Sign of the Cross, blessing yourself with holy water – these all carry a partial indulgence.

● What you should do, then, is the following. Make an intention, *now and in perpetuity,* of gaining whatever partial indulgence may be attached to any and every prayer and pious exercise you perform henceforward.

2. Plenary indulgences
● The Church now limits these, as a general practice, to *one per person per day.*

● You may gain it in *four common ways:*
    (a)   Read Sacred Scripture for at least half-an-hour.
    (b)   Spend at least half-an-hour before the Blessed Sacrament.

(c)   Say the Rosary (five decades suffice) before the Blessed Sacrament. But the Rosary may be said *anywhere* in the case of a family group, a pious association (such as a prayer-group), or a religious community.

(d)   Make the stations of the cross before legitimately-erected stations. No set prayers are prescribed. What suffices is a brief meditation at each station on Our Lord's sufferings.

● *Four conditions* are binding for the gaining of plenary indulgences.

(a)   All attachment to sin, however venial, must be absent.

(b)   One must go to confession within the span of "several days" before or after. Thus a week on either side normally fits this requirement.

(c)   Holy Communion must be received within the same time-limits as in the foregoing. But it must be received specifically for the gaining of *each* plenary indulgence.

(d)   For each plenary indulgence one must recite "any prayer according to one's piety and devotion" for the Holy Father's intention. It is customary in this matter to say an Our Father, Hail Mary and Glory Be.